AUGUSTO BOAL

Routledge Performance Practitioners is a series of introductory guides to the key theatre-makers of the last century. Each volume explains the background to and the work of one of the major influences on twentieth- and twenty-first-century performance.

These compact, well-illustrated and clearly written books will unravel the contribution of modern theatre's most charismatic innovators. This useful study combines:

- a biographical and historical overview of Boal's career as playwright and director
- in-depth analysis of Boal's classic text on radical theatre, *Theatre of the Oppressed*
- exploration of training and production techniques
- practical guidance to the Theatre of the Oppressed workshop methods.

As a first step towards critical understanding, and as an initial exploration before going on to further, primary research, **Routledge Performance Practitioners** are unbeatable value for today's student.

Frances Babbage is Lecturer in Theatre Studies at Leeds U
She has taught and practised Boal's meth
is the editor of *Working Without Bo*
Theatre of the Oppressed (1995).

ROUTLEDGE PERFORMANCE PRACTITIONERS

Series editor: Franc Chamberlain, University College Northampton

Routledge Performance Practitioners is an innovative series of introductory handbooks on key figures in twentieth-century performance practice. Each volume focuses on a theatre-maker whose practical and theoretical work has in some way transformed the way we understand theatre and performance. The books are carefully structured to enable the reader to gain a good grasp of the fundamental elements underpinning each practitioner's work. They will provide an inspiring springboard for future study, unpacking and explaining what can initially seem daunting.

The main sections of each book cover:

* personal biography
* explanation of key writings
* description of significant productions
* reproduction of practical exercises.

Volumes currently available in the series are:

Eugenio Barba by Jane Turner
Augusto Boal by Frances Babbage
Michael Chekhov by Franc Chamberlain
Anna Halprin by Libby Worth and Helen Poynor
Jacques Lecoq by Simon Murray
Vsevolod Meyerhold by Jonathan Pitches
Konstantin Stanislavsky by Bella Merlin

Future volumes will include:

Pina Bausch
Bertolt Brecht
Peter Brook
Etienne Decroux
Jerzy Grotowski
Joan Littlewood
Ariane Mnouchkine
Lee Strasberg
Robert Wilson

AUGUSTO BOAL

Frances Babbage

Routledge
Taylor & Francis Group

LONDON AND NEW YORK

First published 2004
by Routledge
2 Park Square, Milton Park, Abingdon, Oxon OX14 4RN

Simultaneously published in the USA and Canada
by Routledge
270 Madison Ave, New York, NY 10016

Routledge is an imprint of the Taylor & Francis Group

© 2004 Frances Babbage

Typeset in Perpetua by
Florence Production Ltd, Stoodleigh, Devon
Printed and bound in Great Britain by
TJ International Ltd, Padstow, Cornwall

British Library Cataloguing in Publication Data
A catalogue record for this book is available from
the British Library

Library of Congress Cataloging in Publication Data
Babbage, Frances.
    Augusto Boal/Frances Helen Babbage.
        p. cm. – (Routledge performance practitioners)
    Includes bibliographical references and index.
    1. Boal, Augusto.   2. Centre du théâtre de l'opprimé –
    History.   I. Title.   II. Series.
    PN2474.B63B33 2004
    792.02'33'092–dc22   2004004757

ISBN 0–415–27325–0 (hbk)
ISBN 0–415–27326–9 (pbk)

CONTENTS

FIGURES

FIGURES

ACKNOWLEDGEMENTS

I would like to thank Routledge for their support in the preparation of this book, particularly Talia Rodgers, Diane Parker and Franc Chamberlain for all their help and thoughtful editorial advice. I am grateful to Cardboard Citizens and Mind the Gap for generously giving me access to their work and resources; particular thanks to Adrian Jackson and Tim Wheeler for invaluable comments on early drafts. More about these companies' work can be found on their websites, http://www.cardboardcitizens.co.uk and http://www.mind-the-gap. org.uk. Thanks to Bridget Escolme and Jane Plastow, and especially to Marcus Nevitt for encouragement and perceptive feedback on the work in progress. Finally, of course, I want to acknowledge my deep gratitude to Augusto Boal, who has been a constant source of inspiration.

NOTE

In many cases I refer to theatrical exercises or practices within which the gender of the participants is irrelevant to the context. Where pluralisation has not been possible, I have referred to Boal's 'spect-actor' as 'she'; elsewhere I have tried to use 'he' and 'she' in roughly equal quantities.

BIOGRAPHY AND CONTEXT

Augusto Boal (1931–) is unquestionably one of the most important and influential of contemporary theatre practitioners. Early in his career he achieved critical recognition for his innovative work as playwright and director at the Arena Theatre of São Paulo. His now classic text *Theatre of the Oppressed*, written when the repressive political climate of Brazil in the late 1960s and early 1970s had forced him into exile, could be considered essential reading for anyone engaged with the question of whether theatre might be able to effect transformations in people's lives. The flexibility and accessibility of Boal's methods have encouraged widespread dissemination. Theatre of the Oppressed techniques have been applied, adapted and reinvented by practitioners all over the world. Directly and indirectly, his practice has entered contexts as diverse as political protest, education, therapy, prison, health, management and local government, as well as infiltrating the mainstream theatre establishment – and the list goes on.

This book provides an introduction to Boal's work in its various manifestations. The principal focus is upon the Theatre of the Oppressed, since it is this above all which has established his reputation. This first chapter outlines Boal's life and career to date, contextualising Theatre of the Oppressed's birth and subsequent developments. Chapter 2 examines Boal's most famous – and controversial – work of theatre theory and explains its relationship to his practice.

Chapters 3 and 4 focus on the direct application of Theatre of the Oppressed, the former through analysis of **Forum Theatre** as practised by two companies, and the latter by providing a structure for workshop exploration of techniques.

CONTEXT FOR A THEATRE OF THE OPPRESSED

> In stable countries, artists know where they stand – serene and unperturbed. They know what they want and what is expected of them. In a Brazil cast adrift, everything was and is possible: we asked where we were, who we were, where we wanted to go.
>
> (Boal 2001: 264)

It is always helpful to know something of the context in which artists have developed their practice. Sometimes, however, it is essential. Boal is one such case. The body of ideas and techniques that constitutes the Theatre of the Oppressed was not born from purely, or predominantly, artistic decisions and experiences, but grew out of a determined battle to make socially engaged, life-affirming theatre in a climate of extreme repression.

The history of Brazil in the twentieth century is one of economic chaos, instability and unrest. Brazil is a huge country, occupying almost two-thirds of South America, and supporting a population of over 170 million; São Paulo, centre of the manufacturing industry, is the second largest city in the world (after Tokyo). Within Brazil, the gap between rich and poor is immense. Nowhere is this reflected more clearly than in the pattern of land distribution. A 2000 statistic indicated that around 1 per cent of the population owns half the agricultural land (much of it bought for speculation and left unplanted), a glaring inequity which contributes to the country's extremes of poverty and wealth and has long been a source of violent conflict. For much of the century, Brazil has been ruled by a series of military dictatorships. While some of these governments introduced measures intended to redress economic imbalance, the tension between social reform and the need to increase production and maximise profit means that these have frequently been unsuccessful, with the initiatives of one government abandoned by the next.

The theatre practice of Boal and his contemporaries must necessarily be understood in relation to this context. It is possible to identify a series of distinct periods within Brazil's recent history, each with their consequences for the country's cultural development. The 1950s and early 1960s were a time of economic instability, with ambitious plans for industrial development – supported by large foreign loans – foundering on sinking coffee prices. This, coupled with chronic inflation, provoked unrest resulting in strikes and riots from workers and students. The artistic activity of this time was marked by a critical, reformist consciousness, and strongly nationalist sympathies. My discussion of Boal's years at the Arena Theatre of São Paulo shows how the company attempted to produce artistically innovative and politically radical theatre, and especially to foster the work of Brazilian playwrights and establish a genuine 'Brazilian aesthetic', all the while struggling against heavy financial constraints. The military coups of 1964 and 1968 were key points in a period of severe repression that continued, with fluctuations, throughout the 1970s. The power of the (military) government increased with civil liberties correspondingly restricted; oppositional parties were outlawed or refused to participate in the corrupt electoral process. All forms of cultural expression came in for heavy censorship. However, while this period saw the arts under attack, it also witnessed the rise of a theatre actively opposed to the dictatorship in the work of such groups as Arena and Teatro Oficina, both based in São Paulo, and Opinião, based in Rio de Janeiro. The process of redemocratisation began in the late 1970s, with civilian government restored in 1985 and a new constitution formed in 1988. (This was by no means the end of Brazil's economic problems; indeed the late 1980s saw the country's worst recession in years.) Boal was invited back to Brazil in 1986 after fifteen years in exile, during which time he had consolidated the techniques now famous as the 'arsenal of the Theatre of the Oppressed' (Boal 1992: 60).

Although censorship had considerably relaxed by the late 1970s, it has taken some time for Brazil's theatre to recover from its effects. Writing in 1989, Severino João Albuquerque describes a situation whereby older playwrights such as Boal and his contemporary Plínio Marcos (1935–), both of whom suffered the full harshness of the authoritarian regimes, were still recovering from the impact of years in exile. At the same time a younger generation of writers, who grew up in an atmosphere of oppression, had yet to make a distinctive contribution (Albuquerque 1989). In 2001 Weinoldt reflects on the 1980s and 1990s as a period of artistic diversity marked by a shift away

from overt political commitment towards a focus on individual experience, evident in the work of Maria Adelaide Amaral (1942–) and Luís
Alberto de Abreu (1952–), among others. Weinoldt considers that
cultural resistance remains an important feature of the Brazilian theatre,
most notably in the continued efforts to develop genuine alternatives
to mass-mediated culture. The ambitions of Arena, Oficina and Opinião
in the 1960s to create a theatre rooted in Brazilian culture for a popular
audience are carried on by now well-established groups such as Tá na
Rua (You in the Street) and Teatro União e Olho Vivo (Union and Live
Eye Theatre), both of which seek audiences in the poorest areas
(Weinoldt 2001).

AUGUSTO BOAL: EARLY YEARS

Augusto Boal was born in Rio in 1931, son of José Augusto Boal and
Albertina Pinto Boal. His parents were Portuguese, his father exiled
from his homeland in 1914 following his refusal to support Portugal's
involvement in the First World War. José Augusto went back briefly
in 1925 to marry his fiancée and take her to Brazil, but the Boals never
returned to Portugal as a family. When Augusto Boal grew up, Brazil
was under the dictatorship of Getúlio Vargas. The Vargas government,
officially styled *Estado Novo* (New State), was totalitarian in character
yet maintained friendly relations with the United States and other
democracies (Bethell 1994: 7–11). Diplomatic relations with Germany
were broken off in 1938 when evidence was uncovered of Nazi involvement in an earlier revolt against the Vargas government by Brazil's
ultra right-wing *Integralista* organisation, and once the Second World
War had been declared Brazil came down firmly on the side of the
Allies. But whatever the country's declared allegiances, Boal recalls
inconsistencies of behaviour among adults he knew; he notes that
many members of the violent movement *Justiceiros Contra O Nazismo*
(Upholders of Justice Against Nazism) were formerly active within
Integralista, switching their loyalties to ensure they were 'always on the
side of the strong' (2001: 91).

Boal's early years were happy ones. His parents were economically
comfortable and their attitudes liberal. Boal's love of theatre found
expression in shows staged in the family dining room by the ten-year-
old Boal, his siblings and their cousins, and in the first plays he wrote,
using his mother's sewing machine as a table. As Boal represents it,

his attitude then was characteristic of the approach he would later adopt as an adult practitioner. In the staged shows, no individual 'owned' their character; whoever was available to take on a role at the critical moment would do so, interpreting it as they saw fit. On his childhood literary efforts, he comments: 'When I read a story and did not like it, I would rewrite it' (2001: 89), hinting at the philosophy he would later develop in the Theatre of the Oppressed. From the practice of **Simultaneous Dramaturgy**, where the audience have the power to propose developments away from a given script that the actors then concretise, through to Forum Theatre, where they can intervene at any point in the drama, Theatre of the Oppressed emphasises that that which is prescribed – literally, already written – is always open to interrogation.

In 1948 Boal began studies at the National School of Chemistry, University of Brazil. His choice arose from a wish to gratify his father, and an impulse to stay close to a current girlfriend who intended to pursue the subject – a plan foiled when he passed the entrance exam, but she didn't (Boal 2001: 105). At no point did Boal abandon his theatrical ambitions. While doing enough to pass his degree, much of his time was absorbed by his duties as director of the School's Cultural Department, a post entitling him to free tickets at local theatres and opportunities to meet writers, actors and directors. In this way Boal broadened his experience of performance, seeing productions by foreign practitioners as well as the work of Brazilian companies. Equally importantly, he made contacts that would crucially shape his later career. He met Nelson Rodrigues (1912–80), a playwright widely credited with having revolutionised the Brazilian theatre by his experiments in dramatic form and style. Rodrigues introduced Boal to the prestigious critic Sábato Magaldi (1927–), who in turn would recommend Boal to José Renato (1926–) of the Arena Theatre.

IN NEW YORK

Following his graduation in 1952, Boal undertook a further year's study at Columbia University in the US. Seeking to please both his father and himself, he pursued courses in chemistry and theatre simultaneously. New York was attractive to Boal because it presented the opportunity to study playwriting with drama critic, historian and artist-producer John Gassner (1902–66), whom he greatly admired. Initially, Boal's engagement with both New York and his studies was overshadowed by overwhelming feelings of cultural dislocation, but involvement in the University's cultural programme and organisations such as the Writers' Group in Brooklyn helped overcome this. Since many of the artists Boal knew from his time at the University of Brazil were highly regarded in America, he was able to forge further connections. Through his friendship with the playwright Abdias Nascimento (1914–) – founder of the group Teatro Experimental do Negro (Black Experimental Theatre) – Boal met author and activist Langston Hughes (1902–67) and discovered the black literature and theatre of Harlem. The year ended but Boal was not ready to leave, and with his father's support embarked on a further year of study. If the first had been dominated by new experiences, the second allowed Boal to pursue specific ambitions. He combined what he had been learning in playwriting and directing by staging two of his own plays in 1955 – *The Horse and the Saint* and a comedy, *The House Across the Street* – at the Malin Studio in New York, assisted by a group of friends. In characteristically provocative mode, Boal champions the uninhibited creativity of the inexperienced: 'As I was not a director, I had no fear of directing. [. . .] And as the actors were not actors, they were not afraid to act: they were great' (Boal 2001: 136).

THEATRICAL INFLUENCES

While in New York, Boal had the opportunity to see an immense variety of plays and production companies. Given the experience already gained in Brazil, there can be no doubt that by this point he had been exposed to a wide range of artistic influences. It is always problematic to trace the effects of 'influence' on an artist, however. The playwright for whom Boal has probably expressed admiration most frequently is William Shakespeare. As for practitioners, Boal's most evident debt is to **Bertolt Brecht** (1898–1956). *Theatre of the Oppressed* makes frequent reference to Brecht's proposals for an **Epic Theatre**; Brecht's political themes and anti-illusionist, 'critical' production style have found renewed expression in Boal's practice. But, less obviously, his work is also influenced by **Konstantin Stanislavsky** (1863–1938). Given that Stanislavsky's theatre is generally associated with realism, the combined inspirations might seem mutually contradictory. To bring these diverse expressions of theatricality into a coherent framework, it is helpful to consider the education Boal would have received while in New York from the man to whom he had come to study playwriting: John Gassner.

In 1956 Gassner's important study *Form and Idea in Modern Theatre* was published. Gassner's range of reference is broad, as in his other writings. From this, and from Boal's autobiography, it is plain that Boal engaged with work by virtually all major modern European and American dramatists, as well as Shakespeare and the Greeks, and the broad dramatic 'movements' of realism, symbolism, surrealism and expressionism. Equally significant is Gassner's interpretation of the condition of mid-1950s theatre, which he depicts as unstable and eclectic, a crisis born of an unresolved conflict between realism and what he termed 'theatricalism', or anti-realism. Gassner recognised realism as a hugely important and largely positive influence in the modern American theatre, arguing that learning the principles of realistic playwriting — for example, that the main function of dialogue is to advance action rather than be quotable as 'literature' — would lead to better drama. He abhorred 'naturalistic clutter', advocating instead a sharper-edged, selective realism of the kind he observed in director Elia Kazan's 1955 production of Tennessee Williams' *Cat on a Hot Tin Roof*, which Boal also saw and admired (Gassner 1956: 124–5; Boal 2001: 128). But too often, suggests Gassner, the imitative qualities of realism are adopted by playwrights without the driving force of ideas and commitment. In an essay two years earlier he comments that writers were understandably disenchanted with both society and theatre but had 'not yet learned to make anything out of their *disbelief*' (Gassner 1954: 25).

The principal alternative to realism available at this time was theatricalism/anti-realism, but this appeared equally problematic. Gassner applauds the Brecht-inspired rejection of bland realism, which offered no more than a reflection of contemporary life, but argues that the anti-realists had as yet found little of substance to offer in its place. The dramatic forms explored to date seemed to him 'tentative, elusive, or fractured' (Gassner 1956: 141). Theatricalism had most effectively been deployed in the contexts of music hall, musical comedy and vaudeville, he considered; it was least successful when departures from realism became freakish for the sake of it, pompously self-conscious, or too playfully arch.

For Gassner, the necessary invigoration of the contemporary theatre was therefore to be achieved by moving beyond false perceptions of realism and theatricalism as opposed polarities towards an integration of the two in 'active and secure partnership' (Gassner 1956: xiii). In his final chapter, 'The Duality of Theatre', Gassner argues that theatre by its nature exploits both illusion and anti-illusion. Audiences need not, therefore, be given *either* realism *or* theatricalism, but can enter into a performance's sense of reality at one moment and, at the next, appreciate an effect that they know to be 'theatrical' rather than life-like. Equally, audiences can experience something as simultaneously 'theatrical' and 'real'. Gassner sought a creative synthesis. He urged playwrights to consider the full vocabulary available to them, and in so doing to challenge the assumption that certain types of dramatic subject belonged to specific theatrical forms.

It is illuminating to consider Boal's work, in New York and after-wards, in the light of this debate. Certainly, Boal was deeply influenced by realism and impressed by the detailed and disciplined approach to rehearsal demanded by the Stanislavsky System, which he saw practised at the Actors' Studio in New York. He watched some of the Studio's rehearsals as well as public performances and comments:

> Since those Actors' Studio sessions, I have had a fascination for actors who truly live their characters – rather than those who pretend to. To see an actor transforming him/herself, giving life to his/her dormant potentialities, is marvellous. It is the best way to understand the human being: seeing an actor create.
>
> (2001: 129)

The valuing of a broadly Stanislavskian process is very evident here. It is useful to remember this, for while Theatre of the Oppressed is heavily informed by the anti-illusionist principles of Brechtian dramaturgy this does not mean that all tenets of realism are rejected. Far from it: like Gassner, Boal does not make a case for either/or but aims to combine both. The observation quoted is also of interest for the emphasis placed on seeking the 'other' within oneself ('giving life to his/her dormant potentialities'), a principle that would become fundamental to the Theatre of the Oppressed. Finally, if watching an actor create is 'the best way to understand the human being', the Theatre of the Oppressed proposes, by extension, that participation in the creative processes of theatre is the best way to reveal the human being, and through this to understand one's self and one's society. Theatre of the Oppressed does not use performance to investigate matters of social or personal concern simply because it is Boal's preferred medium. Rather, the method is founded on the belief that theatre encourages this investigation because of its inherent duality. Boal's position is close to Gassner's, even though the latter could not have anticipated the direction Boal's work would take. Boal returned to Brazil from New York with a developed awareness of theatre's potentiality, a broadened theatrical vocabulary and an approach to theatre-making informed by principles of actor creativity, detail and discipline. All this is evident in his early work at Arena, and specific aspects would later be adapted in necessary response to an increasingly repressive political situation and as part of his own maturing development as a practitioner.

AT THE ARENA THEATRE OF SÃO PAULO, 1956-71

Boal returned to Brazil in 1955 and was quickly hired by José Renato, artistic director of the Arena Theatre. He spent the next fifteen years working at Arena as director and playwright, a hugely important period in his career abruptly concluded by enforced exile in 1971. The years were also marked by significant personal events; Boal married twice, first – briefly – to Albertina Costa, and then to Cecília Thumim, with whom he still lives today.

EARLY YEARS OF THE ARENA THEATRE

To understand Boal's distinctive contribution to Arena it is necessary to know something of that company's pre-history and particular ambitions. The importance of Arena's role in the development of Brazilian theatre has been widely recognised (Milleret 1987; George 1992 and 1995; Anderson 1996). Arena was founded in 1953 by José Renato. His intention was to provide São Paulo with a professional company which would emulate the ensemble playing, high production standards and commitment to serious drama he admired in the Teatro Brasileiro de Comédia (1948–64), but which – lacking the TBC's financial resources, and having no dedicated performance space – would necessarily operate at a more modest level. Having already staged a production in the arena or theatre in the round style, Renato decided that his new company would adopt this for all their performances. Use of the arena would reduce the necessity for expensive sets, and would mean that touring productions could easily adapt to whatever space (for example schools or factories) was available. Within the context of Brazilian theatre at the time, the introduction of playing in the round was a genuine innovation. Stage design in professional theatre had tended to emphasise artistry, detail and display; Arena's work shifted attention to the organisation of stage space, demonstrating that visually stunning performance was not dependent on high finance. Positive reactions to Renato's early productions of Brazilian and foreign plays (and corresponding improvement in Arena's finances) led to the establishment in 1955 of the first permanent theatre in the round in South America, located in downtown São Paulo, as the company's home.

BOAL AT ARENA: THE 'FOUR PHASES'

Boal's directorial debut was a critically acclaimed staging of John Steinbeck's 1937 novella *Of Mice and Men*. According to David George, the production was characterised by 'social consciousness, "gritty" photographic realism, and Actors' Studio methods', all of which became Arena trademarks (George 1992: 44). Nevertheless, this 'gritty realism' was taking place on a small stage, with an audience on all sides, in a 150-seat theatre. This implies that the style was, of necessity, one of selective realism – as advocated by Gassner – since full scenery could not be used even if desired. Additionally, the close proximity of audience and actors suggests an intimacy of detail equivalent to the film close-up, a strategy entirely appropriate to the ambitions of realism yet one which 'realist' productions on a more conventional end-on stage, in a larger auditorium, can rarely adopt. Boal emphasises the capacity of theatre in the round to stage realism, despite the apparent contradiction that 'the circular stage always reveals the theatrical character of any performance: audience facing audience, with the actors in between, and all the theatrical mechanisms bared, without disguise' (1979: 160–1). In this way, it seems that the Arena Theatre was already finding a concrete expression for Gassner's vision, whereby realism and 'theatricalism' would successfully co-exist.

Boal's description of Arena's activities during his time there demarcates four theatrical phases. These are referred to as 'realist', beginning 1956; 'photographic', from 1958; 'nationalisation of the classics', from 1962; and 'musicals', from c.1964 (1979: 159–66). His account commences with Arena's realist stagings of foreign plays, a repertory explained both by the seeming shortage of texts by Brazilian dramatists and the general, deeply entrenched view that the latter spelled box office disaster. Then, in the late 1950s, the decision was made to produce plays by national authors, many of whom were emerging in the context of the Arena's own Dramaturgy Seminar (*Seminário de Dramaturgia*), initiated for that purpose. The term 'photographic' refers to Arena's continued use of selective realism, but now in a context where the lens turned on the realities of Brazilian life. According to Boal, this second phase – successful in the development and support of new playwrights – was superseded by another in which Arena again staged foreign plays, but ones chosen for their relevance to the concerns of contemporary Brazil and slanted in production to reveal parallels to their audience. The progression from second to third phase was a shift of emphasis from 'singularities [to] universalities', with the fourth phase, of musicals, uniting both (Boal 1979: 165). The most successful production of this final phase, by all accounts, was *Arena Conta Zumbi* ('Arena Tells of Zumbi'), which mediated a historical theme through overtly theatricalist devices, contemporary social commentary and Brazilian popular music.

However, the four-phase account does not tell the whole story. David George's detailed documentation of Arena's output during these years reveals numerous instances that blur the neatness of supposed divisions. For example, the only truly realist production of the 'first phase' (other than *Of Mice and Men*) was Boal's staging of Sean O'Casey's *Juno and the Paycock*, with various comedies and farces making up the bulk of the repertory. Second, the direction taken in the photographic or Brazilian dramaturgy phase was perhaps more fortuitous than planned. The major success of this phase was undoubtedly Gianfrancesco Guarnieri's *Eles Não Usam Black-Tie* ('They Don't Wear Black-Tie'), which opened in 1958 and ran for over a year. According to George, the astonishing popularity of this play, which focused on the lives of peasant-class Brazilians, saved Arena's finances at a moment of near disaster. The decision to produce national writers was taken subsequently in order to capitalise on the success of Guarnieri's play, and the

Dramaturgy Seminar launched as a result. Third, although Arena's musicals are designated by Boal as the fourth phase, the company began staging musical shows as early as 1960 with *Um Americano em Brasília* ('An American in Brazil') (George 1992: 45–7 and 1995: 47–9). The point of making clarifications of this kind is to draw attention to the way in which histories are – necessarily – produced after the event. The four-phase version of Arena's development implies strategic progress through a sociotheatrical experiment, whereas other accounts stress the company's recurrent financial difficulties as the motivation behind many of its decisions. This does not undermine the very real significance of Arena's work, which achieved greatest impact with *Arena Conta Zumbi*.

ARENA CONTA ZUMBI (1965)

Although Arena had indeed been 'nationalising the classics' in the early 1960s, the company's attention was forced back onto the immediate reality of contemporary Brazil when in 1964 President João Goulart was overthrown by an army revolt. If Goulart had liberal sympathies, his successor, General Humberto Castelo Branco, had not. As increasingly restrictive measures were introduced by the new regime, Arena had to reorder its priorities. It now seemed imperative to return to explicitly national subjects, so that recent events could be evaluated and the possibilities of resistance explored. But since realistic dramatisation of the military's activities would attract immediate censorship, an alternative theatrical language was needed. The form Arena developed was a new type of musical, combining Brazilian history, Brechtian distancing and realism (Milleret 1987: 19). In taking this direction the company drew on the success they had already achieved with musical shows, the most important of which had been *Opinião* in 1964 (directed by Boal and written by Oduvaldo Vianna Filho). The concerns of the working class formed the subject matter of this show, expressed through the popular music of the *samba* and *bossa nova* (George 1992: 49–50).

Arena Conta Zumbi was written by Boal and Gianfrancesco Guarnieri (1934–) and directed by Boal, with music by Edu Lobo (1943–). It was the first in a series of 'Arena tells of . . .' shows, followed by *Arena Conta Tiradentes* in 1967 and *Arena Conta Bolívar* in 1971. *Zumbi* is based on an episode in seventeenth-century Brazilian history when a colony of escaped slaves at Palmares was attacked by federal troops, by order of a joint Portuguese–Dutch force, aiming to dissuade further attempts at rebellion. The ex-slaves resisted fiercely but were all eventually slaughtered. With this episode as the musical's basis, Arena was able to recount and celebrate a past struggle against despotism and, through this, offer implicit condemnation of the new dictatorship. Furthermore, the focus on a historical and ostensibly patriotic subject largely protected the play from the attentions of the censor (Anderson 1996: 23).

Ideologically and aesthetically, *Arena Conta Zumbi* was an ambitious production. Arena aimed to reinforce the broadly shared identity of its regular audience – young, idealistic and politically left of centre – by means of historical allegory. *Zumbi* drew vivid parallels between the attacks on the colony and the tactics of the Brazilian military at the time of the coup and later, and by celebrating rebellion in the past sought to stimulate resistance in the present. The aesthetic aims were equally bold. Boal has stated that fundamentally *Zumbi* attempted to destroy all the stylistic conventions which were inhibiting theatre's development as an art form and clear a space for a new system to emerge (1979: 166). This process employed four principal techniques:

1   a break with actor/character correspondence, achieved by having all the actors play all the characters;
2   the use of shared narration – implied by the 'Arena tells of . . .' formulation – to emphasise collective ownership of the history, a collectivity which potentially extended to the audience as well;
3   stylistic eclecticism, drawing on farce, melodrama, music and docudrama, designed to keep the audience entertained and critically engaged; and
4   use of music for its atmospheric and emotional powers, which were then harnessed to reinforce ideological meaning.

Certainly, these techniques were not new in themselves, nor were they presented as such. Boal acknowledges the influence of Brecht, and – less obviously – the drama of classical Greece (1979: 168–71). What was innovative was the specific combination and political application that together made *Zumbi* the first 'Brazilian protest musical' (George 1992: 51).

Critical opinion is divided over *Zumbi*'s achievement. The show was certainly Arena's biggest popular success, initially running for a year and a half and remaining within the company's repertoire throughout the rest of the 1960s and early 1970s, and touring to Europe and the US. The show was well received by critics, though some complained that the mixture of styles created an incoherent and 'chaotic' whole. This charge can be countered, if not dismissed, by recalling that Boal's intention was to destroy existing theatrical codes: thus 'chaos' would be a necessary and expected result (Anderson 1996: 22–6). However, *Zumbi* did not aim to be aesthetically destructive for its own sake but so that a new order could emerge. The production had its own goals but was importantly a means to an end. What came out of the experiment was the **Joker** (or *Coringa*) system, described in detail in *Theatre of the Oppressed* (1979: 167–90). Essentially, this was conceived as a means of presenting a story while simultaneously examining its implications and relevance. Using the stylistic techniques employed in *Zumbi*, the system proposed to use a 'wild-card' figure who could mediate between characters and audiences, comment critically on the narrative and, at certain points, intervene directly in the action. As it turned out, this elaborate and carefully theorised proposal was not wholly successful in practice, possibly because it was too rigid. It was fully realised just once, in *Arena Conta Tiradentes* (1967), a production David George considers 'unwieldy, overly cerebral, and schematic' (1992: 52). But if Arena's aesthetic aims for *Zumbi* were only partially achieved, what of their ideological ambitions? This is almost impossible to measure. As Milleret notes, there exists 'no documentation to confirm that members of the audience really walked out of the performance and engaged in revolution' (1987: 26). She comments that, while it was unlikely the show made a direct impact on political events, it nevertheless contributed importantly by sustaining a belief in the possibility of resistance among the students and intellectuals who formed the majority of its audience. Anderson agrees, noting that, although *Zumbi*'s optimistic tone might today seem incongruous or naive given the subsequent tightening of the dictatorship's hold, it chimed powerfully with the mood of the time which perceived the 1964 coup as a setback but not a defeat (1996: 26).

LAST YEARS OF THE ARENA THEATRE

As the political situation worsened in the years following 1967 it grew harder to voice any form of protest. Arena's activities became increasingly threatened, first by censorship, then by the physical aggression of the military and its ultra right-wing supporters. Boal comments on the impossibility of avoiding partisanship in that climate, even if you were not affiliated to a political body:

> You would be involved in a furtive conversation and before you knew it you had slipped into the armed struggle. A meeting, a secret, and soon the person already felt committed: [...] you had already become a militant before you noticed how it had happened.

(2001: 251)

All cultural activities of the radical intelligentsia were targeted by the dictatorship, but the theatre particularly so, since the alliance between theatre groups and university students had been identified as a dangerous oppositional force (Albuquerque 1989: 87). While modest censorship had always operated in the Brazilian theatre to some degree, it now intensified sufficiently to provoke the theatre community of São Paulo into declaring a general strike (George 1992: 109). In 1968 Arena staged *Feira Paulista de Opinião* ('São Paulo's Fair of Opinions') in the Teatro Ruth Escobar, in outright defiance of the censor's ban. *Opinião* was a show for which local artists had been invited to use their preferred medium to express opinions about contemporary times and debate the role of art in society. It was at this time that the dictatorship adopted more violent measures of control, which took the form of bombs, raids and kidnappings. Boal recalls: 'At the end of a show, actors prepare themselves for the applause. We prepared ourselves nervously for invasion' (2001: 268). Playing concurrently with *Opinião* in the same building was *Roda Viva* ('Live Wheel') by popular singer-composer Chico Buarque (1944–); controversial play in which a pop star is murdered by obsessive fans and the actors pass lumps of his 'flesh' (actually chicken meat) to the audience to eat. In a notorious incident paramilitaries burst in on one performance, destroyed the scenery and beat up the cast (George 1992: 53; Boal 2001: 267).

By 1971 the aggression had reached its peak. The police began to arrest and torture numerous people, including influential theatre practitioners such as José Celso (1937–) of Teatro Oficina, set designer Flávio Império (1935–85) and Boal himself. For three months Boal was held in the Department of Political and Social Order, accused of crimes against Brazil. Boal's rage and anguish during this period of confinement and torture are vividly described in his autobiography (2001: 284–98). The imprisonment attracted widespread attention, nationally and internationally. In America playwright Arthur Miller (1915–) wrote a letter calling for his release, supported by signatures from hundreds of artists from all over the world. The appeal was successful in that Boal was freed shortly afterwards and acquitted of all charges; he was nevertheless sent into exile and, together with his wife Cecília and son Fabián, left Brazil for Argentina. Without Boal, Arena did not survive. For some years it continued to operate as a venue, but the company soon dispersed.

IN EXILE, 1971–86

DEVELOPMENT OF A THEATRE OF DIALOGUE

While Boal was in exile he consolidated the principles and practice which together constituted the Theatre of the Oppressed. Several of his important theoretical texts were published during this period: *Teatro del oprimido* ('Theatre of the Oppressed'), *Técnicas latinoamericanas de teatro popular* ('Techniques of Latin American People's Theatre'), *Doscientos ejercicios y juegos para el actor y el no actor con ganas de decir algo a través del teatro* ('Two Hundred Exercises and Games for the Actor and the Non-Actor Wishing to Say Something Through Theatre') and *Popular Theatre Round Tables* (a collection of discussions Boal had participated in around the world) were all produced in 1974. Boal's work in Argentina and Peru during these years, and – crucially – his engagement with the educational theories of Paulo Freire, significantly informed his pedagogy and hence shaped these writings. Before examining this period, however, it will be useful to summarise the ways in which his time with Arena had prepared the ground for a new synthesis of ideas.

The fifteen years Boal spent at Arena were formative in his development as a practitioner. He had matured as a writer and director; he had experimented – out of necessity as well as by inclination – with numerous strategies in theatrical communication within a context where provocative content had increasingly to be relayed by covert means. These experiments were not always conducted within theatre buildings, or with an educated public. An important dimension of Arena's work – one somewhat marginalised by the four-phase history – was the effort to develop popular audiences among the disempowered sectors of the population. The campaign to 'take theatre to the people' was not unique to Arena, but was associated with the wider *Movimento de Cultura Popular* (Movement of Popular Culture or MCP), an important initiative launched in the early 1960s during the populist presidency of João Goulart and backed by the National Students' Union. Numerous Centres of Popular Culture (CPCs) sprang up in cities and the countryside (the CPC in Rio was founded by Oduvaldo Vianna Filho (1936–74), one of Arena's best-known dramatists). The CPCs' shared aim was one of 'consciousness-raising', but using popular art forms which, it was hoped, would make the educational content of the work understandable and entertaining (Milleret 1990a: 19–21). It was a short-lived experiment – since one of the first laws of the dictatorship that followed the 1964 coup was to outlaw the CPCs (Taussig and Schechner 1990: 52) – and only partially achieved its aims. While the energy that drove the groups made these two years highly productive of publications, films and performances, the CPCs did not ultimately manage to secure their desired audience. An unresolved problem remained in the disparity between theory and practice, manifested in the authoritarian relationship between those who worked for the CPCs (intellectuals, artists and students) and the disadvantaged classes they sought to reach. Relative ignorance about the lives of their proposed audiences, coupled with a failure to appreciate the true extent of their own privilege, meant that frequently 'the famous "message" came accompanied by a great simplification of political and social reality' (Boal 2001: 192).

The story Boal uses frequently to illustrate the contradictions revealed when one community attempts to solve the problems of another in this way is of his encounter with peasant farmer Virgílio (1995: 2–3; 2001: 194). In the early 1960s, Arena toured an agitational play to the poorest villages of northeast Brazil, one condemning the conditions the peasants in that region were forced to endure and encouraging rebellion against the landowners. The show ended stirringly, with the actors (in character as peasants) singing of their readiness to shed blood for the revolution. As Boal recounts, cast members were subsequently embarrassed and humbled when Virgílio, powerfully moved by the performance and taking their seeming commitment at face value, urged them to fight alongside the peasants that very day. As the actors offered awkward excuses – their guns were props that would not fire, they did not know how to fight, they were not true peasants but just pretending – they were made forcibly aware of the hypocrisy of inciting action from a position of personal security. Boal writes:

> Before that encounter we were preaching revolution for abstract audiences. Now we met 'the people'. Virgílio was the 'people' we had been looking for. The peasant farmers of the Northeast were that 'people'. We had finally found the 'people'! *Viva* the *people*! How should we speak to this real people? How could we teach them what they knew better than us?
>
> (2001: 194)

The fast-moving events of the late 1960s, and the struggle Arena faced in mounting theatre of any kind, provided little opportunity for extended reflection on such questions. It was in exile, approximately ten years after this encounter 'which traumatised but enlightened' (Boal 1995: 3), that Boal found himself working in a context where he could re-examine the difficulties it had illustrated so starkly and propose a series of strategies which might be used to surmount them.

THE ALFIN PROJECT AND THE INFLUENCE OF FREIRE

In 1973 Boal left his new home in Buenos Aires to teach on a literacy programme being launched in Peru, sponsored by Velasco Alvarado's revolutionary government. The programme, run by Alicia Saco, was known as the *Operación Alfabetización Integral* (or ALFIN). Its principal objective was to eradicate illiteracy in Peru – a problem which it was estimated affected roughly 35 per cent of the population (Boal 1979: 120). The ALFIN project aimed to teach literacy (1) in the official language of Spanish; (2) in the first language of the participants (in a region where a vast number of different languages and dialects were spoken); and (3) in a range of 'artistic languages' such as photography, puppetry, journalism and theatre. Based in the small town of Chaclacayo, near Lima, Boal organised the theatre strand of the project. His experience is described in detail in *Theatre of the Oppressed* (1979: 120–56), and is considered further in Chapter 2.

The pedagogic principles embodied in the ALFIN project had great impact on Boal's practice. ALFIN's methods were derived from the theories of Brazilian educationalist Paulo Freire (1921–97), though Freire himself was not involved in the programme when Boal was employed there. Boal first met Freire in 1960 when touring with Arena in the northeast of Brazil (the poorest region, where Freire grew up). The older man powerfully influenced Boal's thinking and, indirectly, his practice. Boal has always acknowledged this, and recently paid this tribute: 'With Paulo Freire's death I lost my last father. Now I have only brothers and sisters' (1998: 129). The originality of Freire's work arose from his growing awareness of the disconnection between elitist educational methods and the reality of the lives of the working classes. He rejected absolutely the 'top down' approach to teaching, then favoured by the Brazilian education system, which treated illiterate adults as though they were children. He exposed the power structures at the heart of a system within which students were considered 'empty vessels' waiting to be filled by the knowledge of the teacher. He famously termed this 'the "banking" concept of education, in which the scope of action allowed to the students extends only as far as receiving, filing, and storing the deposits' (Freire 1972: 46).

By contrast, Freire advocated an approach based on the assumption that those being taught were intelligent human beings who deserved respect, not patronage. In his view, the students were not ignorant but simply lacked the linguistic tools needed for reading and writing. He proposed a method based on dialogic exchange, whereby the literacy trainers would learn from the peasants about their lives and through this process the concepts and language that critically informed their reality could be mutually established. His methodology was based on *conscientização* (broadly, consciousness-raising), a process that emphasises the ownership of knowledge. Freire argued that knowledge comes from learning to perceive social and economic contradictions and feeling empowered to take action against elements of oppression (McCoy 1995: 11). His methods proved hugely successful and the Goulart government approved the setting up of programmes all over Brazil, in association with the Movement of Popular Culture. These were considered a serious threat to the old order and were immediately halted following the 1964 coup, with Freire imprisoned as a traitor. He was released after seventy days and 'encouraged' to leave Brazil. He travelled between countries in Latin America and then to Europe, as Boal would do a few years later, disseminating his methods as he did so.

PEDAGOGY OF THE OPPRESSED AND THEATRE OF THE OPPRESSED

The ALFIN project was driven by Freire's argument for the necessity of *conscientização*. The aim was to enable communication in a range of languages – artistic as well as linguistic – without hierarchising one above another, and respecting the knowledge participants already had. The theatre strand of ALFIN adhered to the same principles. In practice this meant that participants would need to learn to 'speak' theatre for themselves, rather than be content to watch plays written and performed by acknowledged experts. They would learn theatrical language based on the need to express their own reality, in order to engage with the contradictions of that reality. Finally, the trainer would be motivated by a genuine desire for dialogue – a belief that in this process the 'students' have knowledge which the 'teacher' needs to learn. This was the approach Boal adopted. Just as Freire had outlined the methods whereby students within the educational process could make the transition from seeing themselves as objects (unconscious and acted upon by others) to subjects (capable of self-conscious action) Boal identified stages by which the spectator – in his view fundamentally a passive being – could become an actor. The proposed steps are as follows: (1) knowing the body; (2) making the body expressive; (3) the theatre as language; and (4) the theatre as discourse. The first two stages are not simply preparation for the more developed dialogue and ownership of the third and fourth stages, as essential principles are embodied from the beginning; the very act of recognising how human physicality is affected by social and economic conditions is one of *conscientização*.

In developing this process, Boal had moved significantly beyond Arena's 'agit-prop' theatre of the early 1960s. In presenting plays designed to rouse working-class audiences to rebellion, the company had adopted an equivalent of the 'top down' process that Freire criticised: they sought to enlighten their audience with ready-made answers, failing to recognise that their behaviour was as manipulative, in its own way, as that of the landowners. Freire comments, in words which recall Boal's reflection on his encounter with Virgílio, that those who support the oppressed but are themselves from a privileged class must recognise and overcome the temptation to fall into patterns of patronage: 'They talk about the people, but they do not trust them; and trusting the people is the indispensable precondition for revolutionary change' (Freire 1972: 36). In his work with Arena, Boal had presented theatre *for* and *about* the oppressed; he had not created a method that would transfer ownership of the theatrical process. The fully participatory approach he now developed aimed to do this.

According to Boal, all the major techniques which form the 'arsenal' of the Theatre of the Oppressed were established during this period: Simultaneous Dramaturgy, **Image Theatre**, Forum Theatre, **Invisible Theatre**. Other techniques, such as **Newspaper Theatre**, had originated at Arena, but were now re-presented as part of the Theatre of the Oppressed system. In his writing, lectures and interviews, from that time and since, Boal has suggested that each technique was invented out of necessity, in creative response to situations for which existing methods had proved inadequate. Invisible Theatre provides a ready example. Here, actors present scenarios based on pressing social problems in contexts where these might actually occur, such as restaurants, shops or public squares. The intention is to provoke spontaneous reactions and stimulate debate among members of the public, who should be convinced of the reality of the event throughout. Boal states that the method was developed because it became too dangerous – not least for himself, since he had already been arrested once – to present controversial material explicitly within the public theatre. The idea was born therefore that issues could be raised 'invisibly', without pre-advertisement and its resulting police presence, and without it being evident who was an actor and who was not (2001: 303–4). Invisible Theatre bears some similarity to the kinds of theatrical experiments taking place in the US in the 1960s, although Boal has been concerned to distinguish his technique from 'a "happening" or the so-called "guerrilla theatre"' (1979: 147). However, it is likely Boal was at least influenced by exposure to such experiments, and possible he reshaped what he saw for a Latin American context, with added ideological inflection. It should be remembered that at the time *Theatre of the Oppressed* was published Boal's sympathies were strongly nationalist, and he was thus keen to emphasise the cultural authenticity of his developing practice. Perhaps here, as occasionally elsewhere, it is useful to look beyond Boal's own account to consider the possibility of a reality that might be less clear-cut, though no less interesting.

ARGENTINA, PORTUGAL, PARIS

The early 1970s was a very active period for Boal. As well as developing Theatre of the Oppressed techniques within ALFIN, he continued to work more conventionally as a teacher, playwright and director. He staged his own plays, including *Torquemada*, written while in prison in Brazil, and a rewritten version of *Revolução Na América Do Sul* ('Revolution in South America'), first presented by Arena in 1960. He continued to travel widely, using Argentina as a base, giving lectures, workshops and attending festivals in Latin America and the US. By the middle of the decade, however, the political situation in Argentina had worsened considerably. Following the death of President Juan Peron in 1974, terrorist activities (by right-wing and left-wing groups) escalated, the cost of living soared and there were frequent strikes and demonstrations for higher wages. Boal's activities were increasingly constrained. He waited over two years for his passport to be renewed, in a climate that became steadily more dangerous: 'When the doorbell rang, I used to tremble until I saw a friendly face' (2001: 312). Eventually the passport arrived, and in 1976 – the same year a military junta seized power in Argentina – Boal and his family, which now included their baby son Julián, departed for Portugal. There they spent the next two years.

The political climate in Portugal – in contrast with Argentina – initially seemed to support Boal's work. In 1975 the military government had moved to the left and 1976 saw the first free elections in the country for fifty years. Boal was appointed artistic director of the highly regarded theatre group A Barraca (The Hut) and among other shows produced *A Feira Portuguesa de Opinião*, following the same principles as the 'Opinion' show he had directed in São Paulo. He carried on teaching, now at the National Conservatory in Lisbon. However, there were continual setbacks. The Ministries of Culture and Education praised the work and promised support, but later withdrew finances and terminated contracts. It was a static and disheartening period. There was still no possibility of returning to Brazil, where the political situation had undergone fluctuations but not substantially improved, and in Latin America generally conditions were little better. Boal's attention turned elsewhere; he accepted several invitations to teach in Scandinavia and Central Europe, but the turning point in his career came in 1978 when he was offered a lectureship at the renowned Sorbonne in Paris.

COP ON THE STREET TO COP IN THE HEAD

While the previous two years had produced no real developments in the Theatre of the Oppressed, the move to France marked the beginning of an important new direction. The enthusiasm with which Boal's teaching of Theatre of the Oppressed methods was received at the Sorbonne led to the creation of the first centre dedicated to its development and dissemination: the *Centre d'Étude et Diffusion des Techniques Actives d'Expression* or CÉDITADE. The Centre trained up teams of facilitators to run Theatre of the Oppressed workshops and conduct Forum Theatre sessions. The techniques began to spread and in 1981 the first International Festival of Theatre of the Oppressed took place in Paris. It was inevitable that as more people began to practise the method, diverse interpretations should enter in. In addition – and crucially, in informing subsequent developments – techniques that had been designed to combat oppression in a Third-World context were now being applied to a First-World reality. While economic inequality and deprivation existed in Europe too (and the Centre continued to work with the poor of Paris), the experiences middle-class participants brought to the sessions were very different in character. Boal was initially sceptical of oppressions which included 'loneliness' and 'fear of emptiness':

> For someone like me, fleeing explicit dictatorships of a cruel and brutal nature, it was natural that these themes should at first seem superficial and scarcely worthy of attention. It was as if I was always asking, mechanically: 'But where are the cops?'. Because I was used to working with concrete, visible oppressions.
>
> (1995: 8)

Recognition that these internalised oppressions could impact severely on individual freedom – for example leading to depression, physical illness and suicide – persuaded Boal of their importance. At the beginning of the 1980s he began running workshops together with Cecília – now trained as a psychoanalyst – to explore the nature of these feelings and ways they could be 'treated' using Theatre of the Oppressed techniques. These workshops were titled *La Flic dans la Tête* ('The Cop in the Head'); the implication was that the old oppressors associated with the dictatorships were not absent from this context of relative privilege, but were operating undercover, subtly and internally.

Throughout the 1980s Boal continued to develop these **Cop in the Head** techniques, adapting Theatre of the Oppressed methods to meet the needs of the changed situation. The modifications were not slight; the term 'cop' might suggest continuation of previous practices, but when the cop was metaphorical rather than actual, it could not be approached in the same way. The established method of Forum Theatre required a concrete oppression, familiar to the whole audience, which could be tackled through a series of spectator interventions. In the western European context the nature of the oppression often proved elusive, or its existence was denied by the individual it seemed to affect most. Such situations demanded methods less public (and potentially invasive) than Forum and increasingly processes, rather than performances, were emphasised. Boal began to acknowledge this new direction as therapeutic. The work has been compared with that of Jacob Moreno (1889–1974), founder of psychodrama, though there was no direct influence (see Feldhendler 1994). In 1989 in Amsterdam, Boal gave the keynote speech at the International Association of Group Psychotherapy's tenth convention. He had renamed the adapted techniques by this time, and in 1990 brought out a new book, *Méthode Boal de théâtre et de thérapie: l'arc-en-ciel du désir* (published in English as *The Rainbow of Desire: The Boal Method of Theatre and Therapy*, 1995).

Critical opinion continues to be divided on the implications of adapting Theatre of the Oppressed in this way. Not surprisingly, the severest challenges came from Latin America where Boal's shift of attention to the 'softer' oppressions of Europe and seeming embrace of individualism was regarded by some as an abandonment of the revolutionary class struggle. David George is unequivocal: '[F]orum theatre now amounts to politically correct psychodrama (US/European style) for privileged groups (e.g., university students and professors) in the "imperialist" countries, who are offered this comforting illusion: all inequalities are equal' (1995: 45).

While recognising the force of such criticisms it is nevertheless possible to offer counter-arguments. That Boal should adapt the methods upon finding himself in a new context with different problems is both unsurprising and entirely in line with the way he has always worked: experimenting, inventing, transforming. The creation of the **Rainbow of Desire** techniques marked a new direction in Boal's work, certainly, but one that could be interpreted as an expansion of original Theatre of the Oppressed proposals rather than an abandonment of principles – a defence further supported by his work on returning to Brazil (discussed in the next section). But it is undoubtedly true that his attitude to his country and its problems underwent a change. Boal was forced out of Latin America. He acknowledges that the extended absence altered him irrevocably: 'No one returns from exile, ever. My country was no more, neither were the people the same people, nor I, Augusto' (2001: 326). This is more than a statement of personal disaffection; it is a recognition of transformed conditions, perceptions and relationships. Silvia Pellarolo interprets Boal's reinvented practice as a positive and creative response to new circumstances. She argues that adaptations of this kind constitute necessary acknowledgements of the changes in sociopolitical structures, in First *and* Third Worlds, triggered by the shift of late capitalism towards globalisation of the economy. The concept of a class struggle, and belief in its possibility, have been destabilised within both contexts and to an extent replaced by wider discontent among all marginalised sectors of society. The expansion of Theatre of the Oppressed, which from the mid-1980s forged connections with many varieties of community activism, such as social work, special education, health and human services professions, is arguably a reflection of 'this new geopolitical and demographic picture' (1994: 204). However, any assessment of Boal's work must consider a further direction taken by the Theatre of the Oppressed, and one which reaffirms its claim to political efficacy: **Legislative Theatre**.

THE 1990S: DEVELOPMENTS IN RIO

RETURN FROM EXILE

The year 1979 had seen a liberalisation of military rule in Brazil; the *abertura* (amnesty) marked the beginning of the country's return to an elected government. This change brought with it some loosening of censorship controls and freedoms in daily life but did not represent a fully-fledged democracy (Bethell 1994). The *abertura* allowed exiles and political prisoners to return to Brazil without legal consequences; it also essentially pardoned those who had participated in the repressive practices of the dictatorship, such as torture and kidnappings (Milleret 1990b: 213). Boal was thus legally free to go back to Brazil from 1979, but chose not to return until 1986. He explains the seven-year gap pragmatically: his family had made a home in France, they had financial stability, and the children were settled in school (Heritage 2002: 157). After so many years of being forced by circumstances to move in a hurry, leaving so much behind, this time they preferred 'to do things at a more measured pace' (Boal 1998: 7). But, such reasons aside, going back to Brazil was not easy for Boal. The treatment he had received under the dictatorship could not quickly be recovered from. Milleret notes that the extreme censorship enforced by the regime was not limited to the cutting or banning of work, but 'could annihilate people's existence or actions by simply not allowing infor-mation about them to be published in newspapers and books, or per-formed on stage' (1990b: 216). Boal had been erased in just this way. How should he reinvent himself after such treatment?

Before his exile Boal had been known in Brazil as a leading director and playwright of the Arena Theatre. He could not have taken up his former position again even had he wished, since the company had long since disbanded and the theatrical climate changed. An invitation from Darcy Ribeiro, then Vice Governor of Rio, led him to return instead as a facilitator to introduce at home the techniques he had developed abroad. Boal was employed to organise the theatrical component of a new programme – called Integrated Centres for Public Education (CIEPS) – directed towards school children from the Rio slums. The programme was one of a number of initiatives launched by the Brazilian government in 1985 under newly elected civilian president José Sarney, designed to improve living conditions for the country's poor. The CIEPS programme provided the children with meals and baths each day, as well as with cultural activities such as music, dancing and theatre, plus their ordinary classes. Boal undertook the work in collab-oration with Cecília, using Theatre of the Oppressed techniques with students, teachers and cultural animators working across Rio state. The programme was potentially revolutionary, Boal believed, 'because if a child leads a human life for a few years she will never accept going back to living the inhuman life that most Brazilians live today' (Taussig and Schechner 1990: 50). But, to the bitter disappointment of all involved, the project ran only a few months. Once re-elected, Sarney imposed a stringent austerity plan and cancelled this and other similar initiatives. Without subsidy CIEPS could not be maintained. But although the programme was officially dropped, the work had taken root. Many animators had started theatre groups in the communities they had visited, and these continued to operate. There was a hunger to take it further. A variety of small projects were undertaken in the next few years. Boal and his colleagues worked hard to establish a permanent Centre for Theatre of the Oppressed (CTO) in Rio, but since they lacked secure funding it seemed that this would have to be abandoned.

LEGISLATIVE THEATRE

The turning point in the CTO-Rio's fortunes came in 1992, an election year in Brazil. It was agreed that the CTO as an independent organisation would not carry on. Its members threw in their lot with the Workers' Party (*Partido dos Trabalhadores* or PT), which under the leadership of Lula (Luis Inacio da Silva, 1945–) had been gaining in popularity, offering to 'theatricalise the campaign' (Boal 1998: 12). The story of how Boal was persuaded to run as one of the PT's candidates for *vereador* (member of the council) believing his candidature to be purely nominal but being ultimately elected – to everyone's great surprise – is humorously related by him in *Legislative Theatre* (1998: 11–18). In the past Boal had sought to avoid party politics, even when the dictatorship had forced its opponents into a political position by default. Nevertheless, his election provided an opportunity. Now, when the CTO groups uncovered problems in their communities that were unhelpfully perpetuated by current laws, a line of communication could be pursued directly to the legislative chamber. Boal could put himself at the service of the citizens, using his political mandate to back changes to the law, or new laws, that they wished to see enacted. Boal argues that, in this way, the citizen is transformed into a legislator – much as Theatre of the Oppressed transforms spectator into actor – and the law-making process returned to the people, no longer the property of an elite. Like the Theatre of the Oppressed, Legislative Theatre is founded on the belief that marginalised and exploited classes desire change. The former aims to reveal and explore these desires and rehearse ways of acting upon them, but the latter 'seeks to go further and to transform that desire into law' (1998: 20). The CTO-Rio found a new lease of life. Instead of disbanding, it expanded its operations, developing a network designed to spread Legislative Theatre strategies as widely as possible.

While Boal has argued that Legislative Theatre, as an essentially transitive process – one based on intercommunication and transfer of knowledge between legislator and citizens – is supported by Freirean principles, critics have not universally found its propositions convincing. Baz Kershaw, for example, rejects Boal's claim that in this process the citizen is transformed into legislator as 'manifestly untrue', commenting that

> the closest the citizens of Rio seem to have got to the actual making of laws was to suggest, through his Council-funded forum theatre groups, that some laws might be more welcome than others, and to sometimes contribute to the framing of them. But to state that this makes them into legislators is like proclaiming that a net-maker is a fisherman even though he never goes to sea.
>
> (2001: 219)

From this perspective, Legislative Theatre represents not an advance from Theatre of the Oppressed's early radicalism but a regression. Twenty years earlier Boal criticised Brecht's theatre because, although the spectator 'does not delegate power to the characters to think in his place, [. . .] he continues to delegate power to them to act in his place' (Boal 1979: 155). Arguably, Legislative Theatre proposes something similar. The Rio citizens are engaged in a thinking process – albeit on their feet – but ultimately 'the power to act' has been delegated elsewhere. Boal's counter-argument is based on his belief in the inherent radicalism of active participation in the theatre process. 'Acting' has always held a double meaning in his work; she who finds the courage to take the space (physical, temporal, mental) to express her reality and rehearse alternatives will see herself as instigator of change rather than victim of circumstances. Equally, according to Boal, legislators have no power of their own but only that which has been invested in them by the citizens; they are no more than vehicles through which the desires of the people can be channelled. Readers of *Legislative Theatre* can consider for themselves how far this method, which claims to use 'performance to make politics' (the book's subtitle), is genuinely subversive. It is perhaps more fruitful here to ask what the impact of Legislative Theatre has been, within Brazil and elsewhere.

The energy and commitment the CTO-Rio brought to the Legislative Theatre project is unquestionable. During the period Boal held office – from 1992 to 1996 – nineteen theatre groups were organised which operated in different parts of the city. Through the work of these groups, with Boal as legislative channel, thirteen laws were passed covering issues from sexual discrimination to the protection of crime witnesses (Boal 1998: 102–13). This is no mean achievement, especially given the political context. From its earliest stages of inception the Legislative Theatre project encountered deep resistance from the right, a reaction that arguably might itself testify to the work's potency. This opposition at first took the form of several attempted legal actions – all insubstantial and ultimately rejected by the chamber – against Boal himself, together with a prolonged and violent campaign attacking the CTO-Rio in the right-wing newspaper *O Dia* in the autumn of 1993. All this is charted in the regular newsletters sent out internationally by the CTO-Rio. A letter dated June 1994 records that Boal's desk had twice been ransacked, his car sabotaged and the group's van stolen. But the letter goes on to recount much more serious events which reveal the wider pressures under which Boal and his groups were forced to work. Two of their colleagues from the Workers' Party had been assassinated in Rio the previous week. At about the same time in São Paulo, two militants from a coalition Party were also killed. In Mato Grosso and Acre, two more supporters had been kidnapped. Subsequent letters report further attacks – physical, verbal, legal – against the political left in general and the Legislative Theatre project in particular. The twelfth and final letter of the series records Boal's failure to be re-elected, in a context where, for the first time in the history of Rio's mayoral elections, no left-wing candidate had passed through to the second round. This turn of events was a major setback to a project that had been considered a success, with finance and political influence swept away at a stroke. In a letter first published in *The Drama Review* Boal described his initial bitterness, but also the determination of the CTO-Rio to continue the work:

At first we were very sad, discouraged, disappointed, melancholic. Ungrateful population!!! Unattentive voters!!! Alienated citizens!!! We had offered our work, our sacrifice, our talent, and we were rejected! Better stop. They don't deserve us. . . . But we are not used to giving up. We decided to go on, to go further!
(1998: 114)

This it has managed to do – at the time of writing, it still operates – despite problems in being once again thrown into a situation of trying to maintain a strategy from short-term contract to short-term contract. The single, direct link to the legislative chamber that existed when Boal was in office disappeared, but was replaced, perhaps positively, by the multiple connections which were forged as CTO-Rio sought the backing of diverse institutions and foundations.

Like other Theatre of the Oppressed techniques, Legislative Theatre has travelled far beyond Latin America. Sometimes, surprisingly, it is even staged in contexts where there is no direct connection to a legal process. On these occasions the outcome of a Legislative Theatre session is the production of purely symbolic laws – unless individuals with legislative powers have been persuaded to attend and can take these proposals from the theatrical to a legal forum. This might seem an extraordinary delusion of empowerment, but perhaps symbolic authority should not be so quickly dismissed. The strategies of Legislative Theatre – some of which are not obviously theatrical, such as the 'interactive mailing list' and the 'participatory budget' (Boal 1998: 93, 115–16) – help to bridge the gap between government and citizens; a gap both actual (when MPs operate without accountability) and metaphorical (for example when voting at all seems futile). If Legislative Theatre changes the way participants see their society and their own role within it, and then – crucially – begin to *act* from that changed position, then symbolic power might yet have real consequences.

THEATRE OF THE OPPRESSED IN THE TWENTY-FIRST CENTURY

INTERNATIONAL IMPACT

At the time of writing – after more than five decades of Boal's working life – it is clear that the Theatre of the Oppressed's influence has been far-reaching. There is scarcely a country it has not touched, whether through Boal's own travelling and teaching or via facilitators trained in the techniques. *Theatre of the Oppressed* has been translated into at least twenty-five languages. In the UK, Adrian Jackson has been a particularly important disseminator of this work; as translator of several of Boal's books and director of Cardboard Citizens (see Chapter 3), he has done much to popularise the methods. Paul Heritage is another who has helped broaden and deepen understanding of Theatre of the

Oppressed, reflecting critically on its application both in Brazil and in the UK. Since the first Festival of Theatre of the Oppressed in 1981, such events have occurred regularly. The seventh International Festival was held in Rio in 1993 (for accounts see Heritage 1994; Paterson 1994; Campbell 1995), and others have since taken place, for example in Toronto, Vienna, Minnesota and Nebraska. There are Theatre of the Oppressed centres, groups and organisations in every continent – such as Jana Sanskriti (Calcutta), Headlines Theatre (Vancouver), Giolli (Italy), ATB (Burkina Faso), TOPLAB (New York), Formaat (Rotterdam) and Ashtar (Ramallah) – which use techniques directly or in combination with other strategies. They have been applied in every conceivable community context to address oppressions of all kinds, and have been adapted and reinvented in ways Boal could never have anticipated (see Schutzman and Cohen-Cruz 1994; Babbage 1995).

THE CTO-RIO: RECENT DEVELOPMENTS

The political climate in Brazil feels more hopeful at the time of writing than in a long time. Earlier this year Lula was elected, making him the first working-class president in Brazil's history, with the famous popular musician Gilberto Gil (1942   ) appointed Secretary of State for Culture. Alex Bellos comments that the latter's new position in the government 'personifies the arrival of the 1960s counter-culture as the establishment' (2003: 10). *Metaxis*, launched in 2001 as the journal of the CTO-Rio, fairly buzzes with excitement at recent, current and planned developments. While Boal continues to travel the world, directing in mainstream theatre (recently working with the Royal Shakespeare Company) as well as teaching and practising Theatre of the Oppressed, he still works in Brazil with the CTO-Rio. By this, as by much else, he demonstrates a commitment to conditions in his own country that refutes criticisms that he has lost touch with the realities of Latin America through 'Westernisation'. Alongside continued practice of Legislative Theatre, the Centre has most recently focused attention on two projects: the first with the Brazilian penitentiary system, the second with the Movement of Landless Rural Workers (*Movimento dos Trabalhadores Rurais Sem Terra* or MST). The former (run in partnership with FUNAP, the organisation which manages the São Paulo prison's education system, and London-based People's Palace Projects) principally involves staging Forum scenes on human rights issues within the prisons themselves, in an attempt to examine the problems that beset the system and explore possible solutions. It is an ambitious task, especially since gaining access to the institutions has proved problematic, quite apart from the challenge of enabling interventions from the prisoners (Heritage 2001: 32–3). The second project seeks to tackle rural poverty in Brazil by backing the MST in their fight for land reform. The MST is a grassroots movement that started in southern Brazil in the mid-1980s and increased in scale and dynamism over the 1990s. In the twenty-first century it has continued to fight attempts to introduce market-led policies that implicitly or explicitly favour landowners. This application of Theatre of the Oppressed is based more on facilitation. The CTO-Rio is working in partnership with the MST to train large numbers of militants throughout Brazil in Boal's 'Jokering' techniques, so that the method can be used by the MST to produce Forum scenes on themes relevant to its members (Santos 2001: 7–9).

THE NATURE OF THE ACHIEVEMENT

While it is self-evident that Theatre of the Oppressed has survived the test of time and gained international recognition, as both a theory and a set of techniques, this does not in itself testify to its efficacy or originality. My discussion of Boal's developing work has identified elements that link his practice to that of others. My impression is that, in the early years of his career, Boal's nationalist sympathies led him to a perhaps over-emphatic denial – conscious or unconscious – of theatrical influences that might have been perceived as 'imperialist'. It is clear, however, that Theatre of the Oppressed techniques are not uniquely Latin American but bear resemblance to diverse practices elsewhere. There are overlaps with Brecht's Epic Theatre, with 'happenings' and the Depression-era Living Newspaper in the US, and with the Psychodrama of Jacob Moreno. Boal's thinking is broadly informed by classical Greek drama, by Shakespeare, Stanislavsky, Marx and Freud, among others. Given Boal's training and travelling, it would be surprising if it were otherwise. In recent years Boal has been ready to explore connections with diverse practices and celebrate what Adrian Jackson describes as his 'magpie-like' attitude to the games and exercises he encounters in other countries (Boal 1992: xxii–xxiii). In this sense the Theatre of the Oppressed – like so many theatrical 'systems' – represents an innovative assembly of ideas from a variety of sources, its distinctiveness principally in Boal's ability to apply, reinvent and codify. But, beyond this, his is a charismatic presence; his writings are lively and persuasive enough, but on hearing him speak or working with him directly it is hard not be won over by his passion, dedication and warmth. Paul Heritage sums this up well: 'His work is valued because it is utilitarian, but it is loved because it promises a heroic vision of what theatre could achieve' (1998: 174).

This leads us to the more complex issue of efficacy. Quite simply, do the techniques work? To answer this in any way satisfactorily, it is necessary to do more than refer to any or all of the numerous anecdotes provided in Boal's books (or in the documentations of other practitioners) of instances where participants learned to see themselves and their world with different eyes. First, the question itself must be examined. What criteria should be used to judge 'efficacy'? What does Theatre of the Oppressed attempt to do? It does not claim to provide answers or solve problems; indeed, it refuses to do so, since this would contradict the democratic principles that inform the practice. Its aim is rather to facilitate dialogue by offering a series of structures that can help make that possible. The Theatre of the Oppressed is intended as a key, but as Boal insists: 'The key does not open the door. It is he or she who, with the help of the key, opens the door' (Ganguly 2001: 35). But for many this is still too abstract a response; the concrete results of the techniques remain in question. How might such results be assessed? To judge the 'success' of a Forum, for example, it might be necessary to take account of the number of people who had the opportunity to witness it; the proportion who offered physical interventions in the action, or who joined in verbally; and who if any learned something from the experience, or modified their behaviour after the Forum as a result. Such an assessment would be beset with problems too obvious to mention, and much of this is in any case unquantifiable. But, even if it could be produced, it would not reveal whether Forum itself 'works', but only how far it made an impact with those people, at that time, in that place. It is more productive to ask in what circumstances, under what conditions, the techniques work best. Theatre of the Oppressed is not one approach but several and this is part of its strength. As the development of Boal's practice reveals, one size does not fit all – the practitioner of this work must make choices at every stage about the situation they are dealing with and the appropriateness of any technique, all the while interrogating those choices.

2

THEATRE OF THE OPPRESSED

Boal's most famous theoretical work is undoubtedly *Theatre of the Oppressed*, originally published in 1974 in Spanish and Portuguese and translated into English in 1979. More than a decade later – a period in which Boal's ideas spread throughout Europe – other writings became available: *Games for Actors and Non-Actors*, *The Rainbow of Desire* and *Legislative Theatre*. These later books are engaging and readable, the propositions persuasive and the application demonstrated through numerous examples recounted in characteristically lively style. *Theatre of the Oppressed* is in many ways a less accessible work. Furthermore, only a small part of it describes hands-on engagement with the theatre process. Given this, many people wanting to practise the methods will turn straight to *Games for Actors*. However, a reading of *Theatre of the Oppressed* will give a much deeper understanding of the principles on which Boal's work is based.

The title of *Theatre of the Oppressed* might seem to imply that the book contains a discussion of theatre produced by and relevant to the lives of the socially disempowered. However, only a limited part of the text directly examines this. The first 100-plus pages provide a critical history of the evolution of Western theatre from classical Greece to the present day, identifying patterns, assumptions, effects and legacies. Boal asserts that theatre always plays a political role, whatever its overt content might be. He offers a political analysis of what it means to be a writer, actor, director or spectator. He insists that all people have both the ability and the right to be active makers of art, and moreover that if that right is claimed it has the potential to revolutionise society. The conviction, breadth of reference and interrogative force of *Theatre of the Oppressed* leads George Wellwarth to describe it as 'the most important theoretical work on the theatre in modern times'. John Arden agrees, urging that it 'be read by everyone in the world of theatre who has any pretensions at all to political commitment' (both quotes from Boal 1979: back cover).

Surprisingly little criticism has been published which deals directly with the main arguments of *Theatre of the Oppressed*, though there has been much analysis of Boal's practical experiments. Given the accolades quoted above, one might expect more in the way of challenges or counter-narratives. Boal has interpreted the lack of sustained analysis of his work as 'critique by silence'; he implies that, for many critics, theatre as practised by ordinary people is deemed illegitimate and hence unworthy of attention (Paterson and Weinberg 1996). However, the lengthy and, at times, obscure route Boal takes to reach his conclusions could provide a different explanation as to why the majority of writing has focused more on the work in practice than on the principles under-lying it. The book's structure might also be off-putting. It may not be immediately evident to the reader that the essays that make up *Theatre of the Oppressed* were not written chronologically but across a time span of over ten years. Boal refers to the book as one of four produced since his exile from Brazil in 1971, but at least two chapters pre-date this (Driskell 1975: 77). Chapter Two was written to accompany the Arena Theatre's 1962 production of Machiavelli's comedy *Mandragola*. The next chronologically is the last in the book – a collection of four arti-cles from 1966 discussing the work of Arena and in particular the production *Zumbi*, which inspired invention of the *Coringa* (Joker) system. Chapter Four describes work carried out within the ALFIN literacy project in August 1973 so must have been written later that year or in the following year when the book was published. Chapters One and Three – the former on Aristotle, the latter on Hegel and Brecht – have no date either, but it seems likely both were added between 1973 and 1974, to clarify the shape of the overall argument. An awareness of this compositional history helps to explain occasion-ally abrupt shifts between different sections.

OVERVIEW

Theatre of the Oppressed claims that originally theatre was a practice shared by all. Boal refers to performance 'created by and for the people', 'a celebration in which all could participate freely' (1979: Foreword). But in ancient Greece this ideal of communal ownership was fundamentally destroyed. First, specific individuals were identified who performed collectively as a Chorus for a passive, watching audience. Later, the playwright Thespis added an actor who interacted with the Chorus and was known as the protagonist (which in modern usage refers to the main character of a drama). For Boal, these alterations introduce two significant divisions. First, the majority of the community are excluded from the creative process, implicitly becoming 'non-actors'. Second, among those who *do* perform, one individual is split off and identified as more significant than the others. These changes reflect one another, since in each case 'the masses' are placed in a relatively passive role. The spectators are now twice removed from the heart of the action, and thus only experience it vicariously. They witness the vain struggle of the protagonist – now, a 'tragic hero' – to resist the inevitability of fate. They observe the punishments that befall Agamemnon, Orestes or Antigone for their diverse acts of arrogance and pride. As a result, Boal argues, the spectators recognise afresh the futility of acting in defiance of the laws of the world as they know it. Theatre has become a tool for teaching them that conformity is both necessary and right.

This repressive use of theatre is perpetuated, Boal claims, in the feudal art of the Middle Ages. Control has changed hands to the clergy and nobility, and the outward appearance of the drama has altered, but the purpose is essentially the same: the indoctrination of values in its audience that support the status quo. The Renaissance theatre, to which his attention turns next, develops within an ideological context where the structure of broadly shared values that had made Greek tragedy and medieval drama meaningful has begun to disintegrate. A new and fiercely individualist emphasis can be identified: the self-centredness Boal considers the defining characteristic of the rising bourgeoisie. But the freedoms promised by this drama are not available to all. The system continues to repress. 'The people' remain an amorphous mass to be controlled by the few, whether the power of the latter is a birthright or won by force.

The first genuinely radical challenge to this system is represented, Boal suggests, by the Marxist poetics of Brecht. In Brecht's drama we see characters who act as they do, not because they are fated to do so, and not because they freely choose according to their individual will, but from their position as social beings with material needs and beliefs which each has acquired through economic circumstance and worldly experience. To understand how and why people act as they do is to understand how such a system can be changed. Boal insists that theatre, which has been used as a tool of social control, can be turned into a weapon for liberation. Brecht's poetics are those of the 'enlightened vanguard' (1979: 155), his Epic Theatre adopting strategies to reveal the mechanisms of a world that is subject to change before spectators who can recognise both this fact and their own potential as transformers of it. But a further stage is necessary in this theatrical revolution. No longer physically passive, the spectators must *act*; only when this is achieved can theatre fulfil its radical potential. We have now arrived at what Boal terms the 'poetics of the oppressed', whereby 'the spectator no longer delegates power to the characters either to think or to act in his place. The spectator frees himself; he thinks and acts for himself! Theatre is action!' (1979: 155). Boal's theatrical experiments in Latin America are offered as a model of **praxis**. Theatre is at last being reclaimed by those who have been excluded from it and used in their own interests – yet these interests are not solely theirs, ultimately, since they support a just society and true democracy.

This, in brief, is the thesis of *Theatre of the Oppressed* and it is one many have found persuasive. Nevertheless, Boal's argument has limits and omissions that may already be apparent and could be thought problematic. First, the depiction of an originary, communal, carnivalesque theatre might strike some as romantic and insufficiently grounded in evidence. Second, in covering such an expanse of time Boal's history is both sweeping and highly selective; he passes over certain periods, but dwells on others judged critical turning points. Third, attention is focused firmly on establishment practice and within this, principally, on 'serious' drama; comedy, which arguably might offer greater subversive potential, receives no special consideration. Fourth, in this account Brecht and Boal – and, of course, the participants themselves – are the chief representatives of theatrical resistance. There is no mention of the forms of popular or 'illegitimate' performance that have persisted over centuries, in various manifestations, alongside the dominant tradition. Boal provides a grand narrative in which theatre was seized from the mass of people and used by the powerful for self-serving ends: now, finally, the tables are to be turned. Clearly this interpretation has great rhetorical power. *Theatre of the Oppressed* is not dispassionate commentary but polemic, Boal's aim being to convince the reader of the legitimacy and urgency of his case.

KEY CONCEPTS

'ALL THEATRE IS NECESSARILY POLITICAL'

This is the statement with which Boal opens *Theatre of the Oppressed*. It is a difficult assertion to accept if we are accustomed to calling theatre 'political' only when, for example, the content of a play offers an explicit challenge to dominant values, or when public production is likely to incur direct or indirect censorship. Much, if not all, of the work of the Arena Theatre could be considered political in these terms. But Boal is defining the word in a more fundamental sense. For him, 'political' implies not a specific position or set of attitudes but the fact of *connectedness* to the system by which a society is organised and governed. All theatre is political – just as all the other activities of human beings are political – because theatre is not autonomous and must thus decide whose interests it serves. Boal's position here is broadly Marxist, though this is not initially made explicit. *Theatre of the Oppressed*'s Foreword provides essentially a simplified version of the theory of 'base' and 'superstructure' proposed by political philosopher and economist Karl Marx (1818–83). This can be briefly outlined as follows: all cultural expressions and institutions of a society (the superstructure) – manifested for example in law, the arts, religion, morality and indeed politics – are contingent upon and determined by its underlying economic organisation (the base or infra-structure). However, it does not follow that superstructural phenom-ena are merely secondary or dependent; they also exert influence on the economic realm, since they are directly concerned with the con-struction of ideology. Thus, in the view of Marx and Engels, the arts cannot in themselves alter the course of history, but can nevertheless play an active part in the processes of change (Eagleton 1976: 10). From Boal's perspective, the statement that all theatre is political therefore conveys the idea that theatre both reflects and affects the way that society is organised, through its dynamic engagement with the value systems underpinning it.

Nevertheless it is important to establish what might be specific to theatre's role here. If all human activity is political, why should this one be of any special interest? Boal deals with this in several ways. Theatre, he suggests, is inherently a particularly 'efficient weapon' (1979: Foreword). This can be argued principally because theatre – as distinct from, say, literature – always occurs in a public forum, making immediate contact with its audience. Theatre is in essence what Boal, paraphrasing Lope de Vega, has defined as 'two human beings, a passion and a platform' (Boal 1995: 16). This description implies conflict, urgency and an opportunity to persuade, emphasising that the art is not static but dynamic. For Boal, this reveals theatre's underlying political function: it presents a 'vision of the world in transformation and [. . .] shows the means of carrying out that transformation or of delaying it' (1979: Introduction). So how has theatre chosen, historically, to show our world back to us? Which conflicts have been enacted, and who has been allowed to mount the platform? According to Boal, the theatre has been appropriated, manipulated and controlled by the ruling classes for use against the people over centuries, in much the same way that the world's material resources have been appropriated, manipulated and controlled. This abuse has been masked by deception: 'Those who try to separate theatre from politics try to lead us into error – and this is a political attitude' (1979: Foreword).

Boal is thus arguing for what theatre is by nature, what it has been and what it must be. In *Theatre of the Oppressed* he seeks to present both an analysis of a historical process of domination and a manifesto for an emergent theatre of the future. If theatre has to date been appropriated as a tool of oppression, it can and must be reclaimed as a weapon of liberation. But, as we shall see, Boal's argument is not that theatre is simply an instrument of propaganda to be used in the interests of whoever takes hold of it. Theatre is proposed rather as a training ground for action.

'"SPECTATOR" IS A BAD WORD'

If, as Boal insists, the entire discourse of theatre-making is political and not merely the content of the drama presented, it follows that to attempt to use it for revolutionary purposes requires intervention at every stage and in all aspects. This is made explicit in the statement that the poetics of the oppressed requires 'the conquest of the means of theatrical production' (1979: Foreword). This phrase adapts for theatre the important Marxist objective that the means of production should be appropriated by the proletariat for communal rather than private ownership. Central to this conquest, in Boal's view, is the necessity of *acting*. In this context, 'to act' carries a dual imperative: theatrical action implies sociopolitical action. It is from this perspective that 'spectator' is a 'bad word'. For Boal, a spectator is necessarily and problematically *one who does not act*. She does not mount the platform – actual or metaphorical – and give expression to a passion, but rather remains 'seated, receptive, passive' (1979: Foreword). From this position, the spectator can observe the dramatic conflict but determine neither its nature nor its outcome. The theatre thus imposes 'finished visions of the world' (1979: 155) onto its audience and purveys received wisdoms. The spectator is forcibly denied the opportunity to participate in an ongoing discourse whereby meanings and choices are open to negotiation.

The insistence that 'liberation' in the theatre can only take place when spectator turns actor will recall the pedagogic theories of Paulo Freire (see Chapter 1). Freire argues that an educational process can never be apolitical, but functions either as a 'practice of domination' or as a 'practice of freedom' (Freire 1972: 54). The former seeks to integrate the younger generation into the logic of the present system and hence bring about conformity. The latter, by contrast, aims to transfer the very tools of learning and experimentation into the hands of its students. The parallels between Boal's proposal and Freire's should be apparent. Theatre cannot be radical by virtue of its message alone. True radicalism comes, it is argued, only through direct participation in, and ownership of, the processes of production and hence in the creation of meaning.

However, a number of objections might be raised to this representation of spectatorship. One is pragmatic: how is this transformation of the spectator to be achieved? What means will be used to overcome passivity, if that is what it is? For many spectators, the phrase 'audience participation' suggests the very opposite of freedom; it is not passivity so much as fear – of failure and ridicule – which has taught them to avoid the front row. After all, if spectators have learnt from past experience that invitations to participate are manipulative or tokenistic, suspicion is entirely justified. For Boal, this difficulty will be overcome if there is solidarity – and hence trust – among all those present at the theatrical event. He would be the first to acknowledge that an approach to the spectator cannot be extended as a passing and limited gesture of benevolence but must be based upon total commitment to the transformation of the theatrical process. Freire's pedagogy makes a similar insistence on the necessity for full and authentic engagement, warning that '[t]o affirm this [commitment] but to consider oneself the proprietor of revolutionary wisdom – which must then be given to (or imposed upon) the people – is to retain the old ways' (Freire 1972: 37).

A second objection to Boal's proposed liberation of the spectator is philosophical, based on a refusal to accept the underlying premise of his argument. What if the spectator is *not* the passive, receptive being Boal depicts, but rather intelligent and discerning – one who might even learn more effectively by observation than through action? This positive representation resembles Brecht's ideal spectator – one who is necessarily 'outside' the dramatic situation, the better to be able to study it (Willett 1964: 37). If the spectator acts, what becomes of the useful critical distance that could accompany the former position? How far is it even possible to evaluate from within? Perhaps for this reason, Boal advocates not so much an abandonment of the spectator role as a reconstruction of it. '**Spect-actor**' is Boal's chosen term: as the name implies, a figure who deliberately and self-consciously inhabits both worlds, observes *and* acts (Boal 1992: xxx). But, since Boal emphasises the importance of the spectator going 'inside' the drama, it might appear that his proposal contradicts Brecht's rather than developing logically from it. However, both practitioners share an underlying aim: to enable spectators to know the reality of their own social situation and of the dramatic action simultaneously. The ideal Brechtian spectator is able to engage with and disengage from that action, but principally at the level of conscious mental process. The ideal Boalian spectator does this too, but with the additional level of physical intervention. For both practitioners it is vital that all participants in the event – 'actors' as well as 'spectators' – experience this form of dual existence, with no one either entirely outside the drama or wholly immersed within it. At all times, participants remain aware of themselves as social beings and of art as social practice. This awareness can only be effectively brought about, both argue, by the careful handling of empathy.

EMPATHY: A 'DANGEROUS WEAPON'

Throughout *Theatre of the Oppressed* Boal is concerned with the nature of empathy and specifically with its misuse and abuse. Empathy can be defined as the ability to understand and share the emotions of another: to feel as others feel. In the context of theatre, the spectator is often thought to feel empathy towards the dramatic character. Of course, some genres are less reliant on empathy than others for achieving their effects. Performances that emphasise spectacular or formal qualities over narrative and some forms of absurdist, surreal or farcical comedy might fall into this category, since all employ stylistic devices that prevent immediate or continuous empathic engagement. But where theatre is principally concerned with the communication of narrative, empathy remains important. This would seem both necessary and inevitable in order to stimulate and sustain audience interest in the action. Furthermore, as Martin Esslin points out, '[w]ithout identification and empathy, each person would be irrevocably imprisoned within himself [*sic*]' (Esslin 1980: 131). Put in these terms, the ability to empathise appears to be an essential quality of humanity as well as of effective drama. Given this, why should it be considered so problematic by Boal and by Brecht before him?

Boal's position on the dangers of empathy is virtually identical to Brecht's. Both condemn 'Aristotelian' drama – by which they mean drama that conforms to Aristotle's dramatic theories, since Aristotle himself was not a playwright – for its emphasis upon a cathartic purging of the spectator's emotions by a process of self-identification with those of the character. Brecht suggests this invites a kind of emotional orgy that inevitably wears down the spectator's capacity for action. Boal agrees, adding that the spectator who consistently indulges in such escapist pleasures becomes content to live vicariously: 'Without acting, we feel that we are acting' (1979: 34). Most insidious of all, Boal argues, is that by losing herself in the dramatic action, the spectator adopts its values, as well as its emotions, as her own. The implication of this is that lessons drawn from a fictitious universe are imposed upon the spectator's social reality, by a process of 'aesthetic osmosis' (1979: 113). In most theatre, the spectator remains unaware that this is occurring but is rather the 'victim, so to speak, of a hypnotic experience' (Willett 1964: 78); she awakes from this having absorbed its messages, but without awareness of the ways in which she has been acted upon.

For Brecht, this negative interpretation of empathy is most closely associated with theatrical illusionism. In other words, the more directly the dramatic world resembles that of the spectators, the easier will be the process of identification. The spectator is invited to take this world as real, and in doing so is not required to consider how its characters and events have been constructed and hence how they might have been otherwise. This aesthetic of seamlessness, Brecht claims, reflects an ideological belief in the world itself as fixed and unalterable; thus the relationship between form and content is itself politically charged, not coincidental. It is for this reason that Brecht's Epic Theatre drew upon a variety of deliberately anti-illusionist theatrical devices, such as slide projections, music, subtitles and clear bright lighting, and employed acting techniques designed to maintain the distance between actor and character as much as that between spectator and dramatic action. The emphasis upon self-conscious theatricality seeks to draw attention to the artifice underpinning characters and narrative. It is in stark contrast to the naturalised representations of 'bourgeois drama' that this poetics of discontinuity is offered. While the first bewitches the spectator into accepting its illusions as real, the second requires that she continually readjust her relationship to the stage action. The formally disruptive, open-ended and internally jarring aesthetic structures Brecht adopted sought to reveal qualities of tension, constructedness and transformability in social structures. Eagleton explains:

> The task of theatre is not to 'reflect' a fixed reality, but to demonstrate how character and action are historically produced, and so how they could have been, and still can be, different. The play itself, therefore, becomes a model of that process of production; it is less a reflection *of*, than a reflection *on*, social reality.
>
> (Eagleton 1976: 65)

In Brecht's model the theatre is no longer a place of fantasy, but rather a testing ground, or – to use one of his own comparisons – a sporting arena, in which spectators are both caught up in the action and simultaneously able to analyse it (Willett 1964: 6–8). Empathy is not eroded altogether but its free flow is inhibited to permit a more detached position from which critical speculation is possible.

Boal pursues the same line of reasoning as Brecht but arrives at different conclusions in practice. His spect-actor invests in the dramatic action physically as well as mentally. Forum Theatre is so called because the space for dissection and debate occurs theatrically, within the frame of the performance itself. As each new intervention takes place, forcing the other actors to improvise and realign themselves in relation to the changing action, the narrative is unmade and remade before our eyes. In this theatre, as in Brecht's, empathic identification and distanced observation exist alongside each other. Yet, of the two, Boal's Forum Theatre is in a sense more reliant upon empathy than Brecht's Epic Theatre and arguably more so, even, than the dramatic or 'Aristotelian' theatre that both oppose. For Boal is inviting spectators to *become* the protagonist – albeit briefly and partially – and, for many, the willingness to do this is dependent upon having themselves 'felt like that' at some time in their own lives. If the spectators cannot identify with the protagonist, they will struggle to replace her effectively. There may be no interventions offered, or those that are may stem from a feeling of duty or a perspective of authority not rooted in authentic experience. This observation might be countered by arguing that a well-researched Forum presented to a well-chosen audience will not encounter this difficulty, and that it is the responsibility of anyone practising the work to ensure that material is both immediately relevant and effectively mediated. Alternatively, it could be proposed that Forum Theatre can be valid even when spectators do not identify closely with a central protagonist. If the established channel of intervention does not prove fruitful, this could lead to the play being opened up in other ways – via other characters, for example – which might even result in a more radical overturning of the dramatic world than had originally been envisaged. Either way, recognition of the complexity of the position of empathy within Boal's theatre is essential. If it is indeed 'the most dangerous weapon in [theatre's] entire arsenal', it remains one that he is unwilling, or unable, to relinquish (1979: 113).

THE THESIS IN DETAIL

These three claims – that theatre is always political, that participation is vital and that empathy is a tool which may be used oppressively or radically – are asserted repeatedly throughout *Theatre of the Oppressed*. They are used as justification of Boal's argument that the ownership of theatre, and hence the right to practise it, has been seized from the masses by the powerful few. They serve also as a rallying cry in the ongoing struggle for theatre's reappropriation by the people. The frequent reinforcement of this manifesto gives the reader something concrete to hold on to within the mass of evidence with which Boal supports it and against the occasionally perplexing lines of argument pursued. But what is the status of the evidence and how valid are the arguments? To address this it is necessary to look further at the gallery of figures Boal draws upon – Aristotle, Machiavelli, Shakespeare, Hegel and Brecht – in order to examine how their ideas are represented.

ON ARISTOTLE: THE 'FIRST POETIC-POLITICAL SYSTEM'

Boal begins his discussion of Aristotle and Greek tragedy with three quotations taken from Arnold Hauser's *The Social History of Art* – an influential Marxist study from the mid-1950s on which he draws frequently. The first states that the Athenian social system, though called a 'democracy' (from the Greek *dēmokratia*: *dēmos* 'the people' + *kratia* 'rule'), was not democratic in the modern sense. Society was governed in the name of the people but in reality was highly imperialistic, its advances bought by slave labour. In this system only citizens could vote – and neither women nor slaves had citizenship. The artistic production of the society, the next quotation suggests, reflects this structure of privilege. Greek tragedy, above all other forms, was its characteristic expression. These plays were seemingly addressed to all in their presentation at public festivals, but propagated aristocratic values through their content. In the final quotation Hauser refers to the economic basis of the theatre. He claims that, since tragedians were paid by the state, any plays whose ideological content ran counter to its interests would 'naturally' not be selected for performance. The implication is that state-supported theatre will itself support the state, since the latter would not knowingly fund its own decline.

Boal's denunciation of 'Aristotle's coercive system of tragedy' which comes next is based upon these assertions. He refers to Aristotle's *Poetics* – the earliest extant work of dramatic theory in the Western critical tradition – and additionally to his *Politics* and *Nicomachean Ethics*, drawing from these a series of ideas about the ethos of ancient Greek society and the role of tragedy within it. In essence, Boal's argument runs as follows. For Aristotle, the function of art was to represent the world not as it is, but as it should be. Drama is necessarily concerned with *mimesis* (recreation). It should imitate nature, not in the sense of copying its outward appearance, but in reflecting nature's movement towards perfection. The human body tends naturally towards health, but is not always healthy; human beings strive to create the perfect state, yet wars still occur (1979: 9). In Aristotle's view, the role of drama was to imitate this tendency towards the ideal, by teaching its audience to love what was right. But, of course, what a society judges to be right will depend on its values and principles. As Boal explains, the values of happiness, virtue and justice are not as straightforward as they might seem since they are based on hierarchies of power. Principally, he claims, the highest 'justice' for the Greeks was embodied in their own constitution; this effectively excludes the possibility of challenging established laws. Happiness for citizens comes from upholding the constitution; to do this they must live rationally and virtuously, and virtue depends upon observing moderation in all things.

Boal's argument is that the role of theatre in general, and tragedy in particular, was to indoctrinate its spectators with belief in the essential rightness of the status quo. The key to the effectiveness of the system is the operation of empathy. The spectators identify with the play's tragic hero. They recognise their own failings in the character flaw, or *humartia*, which he exhibits and which brings him into conflict with the social ethos. Ultimately, through his eventual fall and recognition of his error, the spectators are brought to reject anti-social elements within themselves, 'purged' of them in the process of catharsis. According to Boal, this is how Aristotle states that tragedy should operate and to pursue this end has constructed what is effectively 'the first, extremely powerful poetic-political system for intimidation of the spectator, for elimination of the "bad" or illegal tendencies of the audience' (1979: Introduction).

This representation of the *Poetics'* role needs some qualification. First, since Aristotle was born in 384 BCE he was not a contemporary of the fifth-century tragedians whose plays he discusses. This means that his *Poetics* is better understood as an analysis of tragedy from the perspective of a philosopher than a set of instructions for its composition. In addition, although the *Poetics* has exerted huge influence on theorists and critics since the Renaissance, it was not widely known in antiquity (Aristotle 1996a: vii–viii). Given this, it seems unlikely that it would have operated as a controlling force in Aristotle's own time. Happiness, virtue and justice were certainly integral to the Athenian social ethos and a reading of the *Nicomachean Ethics* – though not of the *Poetics*, which has little on this – provides evidence to support Boal's interpretation of these concepts. However, one could select elements from the same source that would modify or contradict his reading. Aristotle does argue that happiness arises from acting virtuously and rationally, but he also observes that it is dependent upon material prosperity since 'it is impossible, or at least not easy, to play a noble part unless furnished with the necessary equipment' (Aristotle 1996b: 16). Here, virtue is not wholly separated from economic issues. Furthermore, though Aristotle criticises extremes of behaviour, it does not follow that moderation equals docility. He emphasises the importance of achieving balance in one's responses, located somewhere between excess and deficiency. Among his examples he includes 'courage', 'greatness of soul' and 'righteous indignation', none of which imply conformity (1996b: 32). Finally, Aristotle's account of the just constitution – coming from a position which assumes slavery, anti-feminism, imperialism and xenophobia as natural and necessary – of course differs markedly from modern, more liberal conceptions. He also continues from this premise to argue that laws which are in accordance with this just constitution will themselves necessarily be just (Aristotle 1995: 84–119). Yet, while Boal's extractions from Aristotle are accurate in themselves, his conclusion that 'happiness consists in obeying the laws' is perhaps reductive.

There is too little evidence for us today to know conclusively whether Greek tragedy operated as 'coercively' as Boal suggests. The plays as a body do assert the need to maintain order, which supports the idea that their underlying ethos is conservative. Boal's critique relies upon specific readings of two concepts: *hamartia* and catharsis. Both of these have been debated by critics at great length and there is insufficient space here to do justice to the complexity of their discussions (see Halliwell 1986; Rorty 1992; Andersen and Haarberg 2001). Boal interprets *hamartia* as a flaw, a socially undesirable behavioural extreme that ultimately brings about the hero's downfall. The spectators empathise with the hero but are terrified by his fate, and thus are purged of their own extreme impulses. However, *hamartia* has been understood by many critics to mean not 'flaw' but 'error', one that might result from ignorance of some circumstance or fact. An example would be Oedipus' ignorance of the identity of his parents, which leads him to kill his father and marry his mother. This reading is implicitly backed by Aristotle's statement in the *Poetics* that the change from good to bad fortune which the hero undergoes is 'not due to any moral defect or depravity, but to a [*hamartia*] of some kind' (Aristotle 1996a: 21). In other words, *hamartia* must be distinct from anti-social vice.

In Boal's analysis, Oedipus' *hamartia* is not ignorance but the pride that initially leads him to glory but through which he is eventually destroyed. According to his thesis, the spectators of this tragedy would have their own excesses of pride purged through empathic association with the protagonist. But even if Oedipus' *hamartia* is interpreted as pride – and certainly Boal is by no means the only critic to read the play in this way – we might question the reasoning. If this is propaganda, it is highly cryptic. After all, people are not normally in the habit of killing their fathers and marrying their mothers; it seems oddly convoluted to attempt to teach a general lesson by such a specific example. Additionally, since Aristotle states that the hero should be of high status, 'distinguished' and enjoying 'great good fortune' (1996a: 21), it might be thought unlikely that those in the audience with the least social power – with whom Boal, as a Marxist, is most concerned – would identify with this figure so directly.

Aristotle himself does not argue that it is the *hamartia*, however defined, which is to be removed. At one point he states clearly that the action of tragedy provokes responses of pity and fear in the spectators and that these are the emotions to be purged through a process of catharsis (Aristotle 1996a: 10). 'Catharsis' is another term that has been variously understood, but it is usually thought to carry meanings of both purgation and purification. For example, Aristotle comments in the *Politics* that music can be cathartic, suggesting that people with hysterical tendencies can obtain 'pleasurable relief' by listening to music which actually stimulates frenzy (Aristotle 1995: 315–16). The principle implied is homeopathic: exposure to a small dose of a specific irritant – here in an artistic, mediated form – is thought to exercise a healing effect on those prone to experience it as a disease. As with the virtues, Aristotle is seeking to counteract excess (or deficiency) and thus achieve a healthy balance. If tragic drama stimulates responses in the spectators of pity for the protagonist and of fear, on observing his fate, as Aristotle suggests it does, then the possible cathartic effect might be to reduce or revive the spectators' capacities for these feelings. By contrast, Boal interprets catharsis as the removal of 'impurities'. His argument is that pity and fear 'have never been vices or weaknesses or errors and, therefore, never needed to be eliminated or purged' (Boal 1979: 31). This leads him to propose, contentiously, that catharsis is seeking to destroy something else, 'something which threatens the individual's equilibrium and consequently that of society [. . .] something *directed against the laws*' (1979: 31–2).

We might not accept every stage of Boal's reasoning in this first chapter, but the picture he outlines, of theatre used by the state – whether overtly or more subliminally – to reinforce dominant ideology, is nevertheless recognisable. The urgency of the debate comes from the insistence that, according to Boal, the 'Aristotelian system' is not historically remote but has survived to this day. We can see it perpetuated in all those plays, films and television dramas which teach that the dominant values of a given society are ultimately stronger than the will of the individual who refuses, or is unable, to accept them. Boal's example is the 'Western' film, which he suggests typically teaches that the aggressively non-conformist anti-hero who controls a town will in the end always be defeated by the forces of approved law and morality; we may admire him as he has his day, but understand that this can only be a temporary departure from the order which will always, finally, be reasserted.

The same principles Boal identifies are also widespread in the theatre. It is arbitrary to refer to specific plays, especially since Boal is claiming that the 'system' is pervasive rather than reappearing at isolated moments, but a single illustration may nevertheless be helpful. In *An Enemy of the People* (1882) by Henrik Ibsen (1828–1906), the protagonist Dr Stockmann discovers that the town spa is sourced by tainted water that is causing users to become ill. He insists it be closed until the problem is solved, but is met by opposition on all sides since the spa has generated considerable wealth for the townspeople and they are unwilling to see this compromised. Everyone unites against Stockmann to destroy his credibility, family and livelihood: he is declared an 'enemy of the people'. Ibsen's play is offered as critique, the theme of disease implying social corruption as much as physical debilitation. But Boal's analysis, if applied to this work, would suggest that, even though the drama reveals the society in question to be deeply flawed and appears to challenge this, its *ultimate* message is that such attempts meet with failure. The 'indoctrination' might even be more subtly effective given that it is the people themselves, not simply individual authority figures, who refuse to allow change.

There are of course exceptions to the schema that Boal outlines. His concern, however, is to draw attention to a tendency in drama to follow what he terms the 'Aristotelian system', which has at its heart the aim of adjusting the individual to what pre-exists. But even beyond this argument about the ideological content and structuring of drama is the problem, as Boal sees it, that the *production* of theatre remains exclusive. Only those designated as 'artists' can create; the rest of us are passive spectators – non-artists unable to give shape to our visions. Thus the fundamentals of this theatre are at fault, Boal insists, and if 'we want to stimulate the spectator to transform his society, to engage in revolutionary action, in that case we will have to seek another poetics' (1979: 47). The essence of this declaration – that revolutionary ambitions demand revolutionary means – is more straightforward and arguably more persuasive than the evidence that has been used to arrive at it.

ON MACHIAVELLI, SHAKESPEARE AND THE RISE OF THE BOURGEOISIE

The opening sections of Boal's second chapter concentrate upon the drama of the Middle Ages. The society of the time was largely feudal, a system whereby ordinary people held land in exchange for allegiance to a member of the nobility. This culture, Boal suggests – further dominated by the influence of the Church – was characterised by super- stition, widespread illiteracy and an 'almost total absence' of commerce (1979: 54–5). Within this context the theatre continues to be appro- priated for purposes of moral and social control, this time under the joint influence of clergy and aristocracy; 'transcendent' values are emphasised over and above attention to immediate material conditions. Boal represents the drama of this period as both a continuation of the 'Aristotelian system' and a transformation of it. It is continued, in that the aim remains to 'immobilise society' by reinforcing the values of the status quo; it is transformed by an overt didacticism which saw characters become abstractions of moral and religious principles – such as Lust, Sin or the Devil – and narratives serve as demonstrations in which 'the good were rewarded and the bad were punished' (1979: 55–7). This picture of course gives only the broadest outlines; no reference is made for example to the more light-hearted and satirical alternatives to religious drama that were also available (Happé 1999; Walker 2000).

Boal describes the development of Western theatre from classical tragedy to medieval drama as a history of control exercised by more-or-less stable political systems marked by a clearly defined social ethos. ('Stability' is a relative term, however, and historians might well contest this overview.) The major disruption to this comes about, he argues, with the Renaissance. The key influences leading towards the change are identified as the growth of commerce and accompanying idea of profit, and the new humanist emphasis following the Reformation which challenged the doctrines and practices of the medieval church and ultimately led to the freedom of dissent. These provide the context and impetus for the rise of the bourgeoisie: the new 'middle class' – neither peasant nor aristocrat – which had begun to emerge in the medieval period but whose power was consolidated during the sixteenth and seventeenth centuries. The theatre of this period both reflected and reinforced these changes, Boal argues. The two playwrights used as illustrations are Niccolò Machiavelli (1469– 1527) – better known as a proponent of political advice – and William Shakespeare (1564–1616). In the work of both dramatists Boal sees the concept of 'character' evolving, with figures created who are no longer essentially abstractions of values as they had tended to be in the medieval theatre. For him, Machiavelli's *Mandragola* ('The Mandrake Root', 1518) is a transition play, its characters 'not yet human beings completely individualised [but] no longer mere symbols and signs'; by contrast, Shakespeare's characters – close to a century later – are multi-dimensional, revealing 'man in all his plenitude' (1979: 66, 63). In the work of these authors, although to different degrees, the protagonists tend to be self-interested and self-absorbed. Their guiding principles, Boal suggests, are *virtù* and praxis. *Virtù* – a term drawn from Machiavelli's political philosophy – is explained by him as the individual's enterprising spirit, ability and initiative. Praxis represents the necessity for action: '[r]ight and wrong, good and bad – these can be known only in relation to practice' (1979: 61). The fate of these new protagonists is not predetermined by God, or gods, nor are they mere instruments in an eternal struggle between good and evil. They believe in their own power to realise their ambitions, surmounting any obstacles that lie in their path. They are beings capable of making free choices. Boal sums up the change that has occurred in this way: 'What happened to the character in theatre? He simply ceased to be an object and became a subject of the dramatic action. The character was converted into a bourgeois conception' (1979: 63). Boal invites us to see the rise of the bourgeoisie – the new dominant class – reflected in this drama. Both the new independence its characters display and the values to which they subscribe are 'bourgeois' constructions. Machiavelli is the initiator of this 'new poetics', while Shakespeare develops this to the extent that he can be considered 'the first bourgeois dramatist' (1979: 58, 64).

In essence Boal's schema follows the analysis of Marx. One 'mode of production', feudalism, is replaced by another, capitalism (see Marx and Engels 1992: 3–16). With this change comes individualism, which favours self-reliance and independence of action as opposed to state control. This interpretation of history is not universally accepted. Alan Macfarlane's *The Origins of English Individualism* (1978), for instance, offers a radical anthropological perspective which challenges perceptions of early 'peasant' society as tradition-directed, arguing that what we think of as individualism in fact comes into being several centuries before the Renaissance. Boal's representation of theatrical change could also be problematised. The idea of the dramatic character was transformed in this period in broadly the way he describes. Nevertheless, the perception of Shakespeare's characters as multidimensional subjects who display a new 'interiority' has been countered by many critics, who have suggested that these figures are more firmly rooted in morality drama than humanist readings generally acknowledge (see Belsey 1985; Maus 1995). However, the degree to which these characters – or, indeed, those of Machiavelli – are recognisable as individualised subjects is less crucial to Boal's argument than the assertion that the plays are demonstrations of new 'bourgeois' values. As Milling and Ley observe, '[a]ny Marxist historical scheme will be searching for capital and the bourgeoisie in the origins of the modern era' (2001: 156) and in his discussion of the two playwrights Boal pursues some unexpected lines of reasoning. In his analysis of *Mandragola*, the two characters that for Boal most clearly exhibit the 'defining' bourgeois quality of *virtù* are Ligurio the parasite and Friar Timoteo, neither of whom is actually bourgeois in status. At the same time the most obviously bourgeois character, the foolish lawyer Messer Nicia, is patently presented as an object of ridicule. This means that Boal is separating what he had termed 'bourgeois values' from bourgeois characters. This

strategy reappears in his discussion of Shakespeare, where he acknowledges that in almost all cases the protagonists are in fact drawn
from the nobility. His argument is that the 'bourgeois nature of the
works of Shakespeare is not to be found in their externals at all, but
only in the presentation and creation of characters endowed with *virtù*
and confident in praxis' (1979: 64). At such moments Boal's analysis
appears overly driven by the determination to arrive at a desired
conclusion.

Boal proposes that in this period the clergy and nobility controlled
the theatre in much the same way as the wealthy did in ancient Greece.
In both cases, audiences are taught – through a process of empathic
identification and catharsis – to perceive their immediate needs or
desires as immaterial in relation to a 'greater good'. But in this emergent 'bourgeois' drama, as Boal terms it, previously upheld moral
certainties are overturned. The new dominant ideology – necessarily
reflected in dominant theatre practice – emphasises freedom of action,
initiative and achievement. The apparent radicalism of this change might
seem to promise more liberating and inclusive possibilities for theatre
than those offered by preceding systems, but the point of Boal's argument is precisely that this does *not* happen. The exalted, multi-
dimensional dramatic subject who can speak and claim power is no
'universal' human being but a limited and exclusive bourgeois conception. In this new theatre 'the people either remain in the background
or are easily fooled and passively accept the change of masters' (1979:
65); in other words, they are as far from being active agents as in the
Greek theatre. Catherine Belsey similarly interrogates the identity of
the new character-subject, commenting that

> the 'common-gender' noun largely failed to include women in the range of its
> meanings. Man is the subject of liberal humanism. Woman has meaning in
> relation to man. And yet the instability which is the result of this asymmetry is
> the ground of protest.
>
> (1985: ix)

While Belsey's analysis is principally gender- rather than class-directed,
like Boal she is concerned with the limits of the dramatic subject who
emerged from this period. To be a subject is to be able to speak, to
participate in the making of meanings. The point both Boal and Belsey
make is that not only are 'other' subjectivities excluded from this

process, but the very nature of liberal humanist discourse disguises this by seeming to represent – democratically – the voice of all. But equally, and crucially, both Boal and Belsey highlight this ideology as inherently unstable: this means that it is vulnerable to attack.

ON HEGEL AND BRECHT: POETICS OF HARMONY AND DISRUPTION

Boal's discussion of German philosopher Georg Wilhelm Friedrich Hegel (1770–1831) begins towards the end of his chapter on Machiavelli in an essay entitled 'Modern Reductions of Virtù' (1979: 73–9). This provides a selective overview of artistic movements from the eighteenth, nineteenth and twentieth centuries. Boal focuses on how these influenced the theatre, arguing that they can be seen as preservations of bourgeois values and simultaneously as adaptations or 'reductions' of these. In his view, Shakespeare's plays had analysed man multidimensionally – politically, metaphysically, philosophically, romantically – even though it was the exceptional man, rather than all men (or indeed women), who was dramatised. But after Shakespeare, he claims, that same man is diminished in various ways. Romanticism does this by retreating from the 'sordid' material world into the spiritual realm of the imagination. Realism does this by assuming a pseudo-scientific objectivity which – hiding the author's actual subject-position – can only reproduce that which is 'supposedly already known'. Absurdism does this by creating 'anti-theatre'; Boal's example here is playwright Eugène Ionesco (1912–94), who 'tries to take away from man even his powers of communication'. All these are seen as reductions since they close down the potential multidimensionality of the dramatic subject, dehumanising the character that had been created (1979: 75–8). At the same time, they represent a series of ways of abdicating from any form of political or ethical commitment. Boal implies that Romanticism seeks to rise above material issues, realism provides only amoral observation, while Absurdism rejects even the possibility of debate.

The purpose of Boal's essay is evidently to demonstrate lines of continuity in the history of Western theatre. While it has 'evolved', theatre has remained a tool in the hands of the dominant social group, reinforcing the ideology of that group even when seemingly apolitical in content. As part of its coercive project, Boal argues, it has consistently denied individuality and autonomy to the poorer classes, who from the perspective of the powerful are simply the 'masses': the uncivilised lumpenproletariat. This is not the only way theatrical history can be interpreted, but it is a persuasive reading which is reflected elsewhere in Marxist criticism, for example in the work of Antonio Gramsci (1891–1937), Louis Althusser (1918–90) and Raymond Williams (1921–88). But distinctive to Boal's discussion, both in this section and in the third chapter of the book, is his attribution of responsibility to Hegel for closing down the 'unknown, and possibly dangerous, directions' in which the dramatic subject might otherwise have travelled (1979: 73).

The work of Hegel will be more familiar to students of philosophy than theatre. Given this, it may seem surprising that Boal should devote as much space to Hegel's ideas as he does and insist so vehemently on their importance. The reason is that Boal seeks to *expose* Hegel as the conservative force who successfully imposed limits on the newly acquired freedoms of the dramatic character, ensuring instead 'that the dogmatic pre-established truth would prevail' (1979: 73). In his view, Hegel is a crucial shaper of the modern understanding of theatre, his values filtering through into contemporary consciousness without our direct knowledge. Boal takes issue with these values in several ways. As with his discussion of Aristotle, Boal draws from his subject's wider philosophical writings, as well as those that relate directly to the dramatic, in order to develop his hypothesis.

A central element of Hegel's philosophy is his conception of what it means for human beings to be free and his perception of world history as 'the progress of the consciousness of freedom' (Singer 2001: 33). For Hegel, freedom is not fundamentally about the absence of tyranny, nor is it to do with independent freedom of choice. Freedom comes rather from acting in accordance with reason. The faculty for rational thought, he believes, is shared by all human beings. A society whose every principle and institution is founded upon reason will be a society to which every human being will freely conform as an expression of his or her own rational will. It follows that for Hegel '[o]ur duty and our self-interest will then coincide, for our duty will be rationally based, and our true interest is to realise our nature as a rational being' (Honderich 1995: 341). Boal suggests that the implication of Hegel's argument is that 'freedom' ultimately consists in doing one's duty. The insistence upon reason, combined with the reinforcement of ethical values represented as universally shared and natural – as opposed to socially determined and specific – provides a seemingly logical and democratic basis from which to defend staunchly conservative principles (1979: 73–4).

From this discussion of freedom, Boal turns to Hegel's analysis of theatre as outlined in *The Philosophy of Fine Art* (1920 [1835]). From the three essays in which he summarises Hegel's perception of the dramatic – 'Types of Poetry in Hegel', 'Characteristics of Dramatic Poetry, Still According to Hegel' and 'Freedom of the Character-Subject' (1979: 86–91) – two points should be highlighted. The first relates to the nature of tragedy. Boal asserts that for Hegel 'true tragedy' arises from the collision of irreconcilable forces or values, not of good and bad, just and unjust, but each one deserving in itself. However, tragedy must conclude in equilibrium. Since reconciliation of these forces is an impossibility, the resolution of the dramatic conflict must be brought about by the re-establishment of harmony, overriding all opposing claims and dismissing as ultimately irrelevant all questions of individual guilt, innocence, justice or need. This summation of Hegel's position recalls Boal's earlier discussion of Aristotle. Here, as before, Boal argues that the underlying ambition of tragedy is one of 'purging the spectator's anti-establishment characteristics' (1979: 106). Once again, empathy is the chief means by which this is achieved.

The second major point made by Boal is about character. According to Hegel, he states, those who embody the dramatic conflict must themselves be 'free'. In other words, the collision must proceed from individual volition rather than external conditions. If Sophocles' *Antigone* is taken as an example, Creon's refusal to allow Antigone's traitorous brother an honourable burial, opposed by Antigone's determination that the burial take place in defiance of his ruling, can be understood as a clash of two ethical principles: the good of the state versus the good of the family. As Boal explains, for Hegel these characters are not simply two individuals reacting to external occurrences but concretions of moral values in themselves. The circumstances of the conflict permit the fullest expression of their essential nature (Hegel 1920: 251). If all 'exterior' events have their origin in the character's 'interior' spirit, in this poetics, Boal claims, 'the character is the absolute *subject* of his actions' (1979: 88). In this way he prepares the ground for the fundamental opposition he is seeking to set up between the 'idealist' poetics of Hegel, on the one hand, and the 'materialist' poetics of Brecht, on the other. In the former, he insists, the dramatic character is seen as a free and self-determining subject; in the latter, the character is always on one level the object of social forces and therefore '*not free* at all' (1979: 92).

A problem with Boal's argument here is the implication that Hegelianism and Marxism are diametric opposites. According to Boal, Brecht's 'Marxist poetics' are 'basically an answer and a counter-proposal to the idealist poetics of Hegel', with Brecht himself '*squarely, totally, globally opposed* to Hegel' (1979: 84, 93). Boal includes in *Theatre of the Oppressed* an adapted version of Brecht's table charting changes of emphasis between the dramatic theatre and his own Epic Theatre (1979: 95). However, the way it is presented creates the impression that Brecht was self-consciously reacting against specifically Hegelian poetics, when in reality there is no evidence to suggest that this is the case and some which indicates rather that Brecht appreciated Hegel's work (Willett 1964: 37; Esslin 1980: 151–2; Milling and Ley 2001: 163). Furthermore, in establishing this set of philosophical – as well as theatrical – polarities, Boal does not acknowledge the extent to which Marx admired and was directly indebted to Hegel. While Marx departed from Hegelian thought on many points, his own philosophy was a deliberate attempt to marry the tradition of German idealism epitomised by Hegel with the 'materialistic' science of political economy. Allen Wood comments that Hegel and Marx shared a view of modern culture 'as both a scene of "alienation" for human beings from themselves, their lives, and others, and also as holding out the promise of the conquest or overcoming of alienation' (Honderich 1995: 524). The crucial difference between them was one of approach. Hegel believed that the project of self-fulfilment and communal reconciliation was principally philosophical/spiritual, while Marx saw it as fundamentally socioeconomic. This distinction is clearly important, but does not fully explain the either/or dynamic Boal sets up which places all figures within his schema in more extreme positions than they themselves would probably have chosen.

Brecht's proposals for an Epic Theatre represent in Boal's view an absolute reversal of the reactionary and repressive aspects of the dominant dramatic tradition. The external action of the Epic Theatre is determined by social forces, not the free will of characters. The goal of the drama is the exposure and ultimately the transformation of society's contradictions, not their justification. The ending must be one of disequilibrium and lack of resolution rather than harmony, since the theatrical event urges the beginning of action instead of showing its conclusion. Finally, in this entire process the tendency towards empathy is disrupted rather than encouraged in order that the spectator leave the theatre not cathartically soothed but appalled by the vision of the world she has seen and thus stirred to change it. For Boal, Brecht's theatre, developed during the first half of the twentieth century – or at least, his proposals for the theatre, since these were not fully realised in practice – constitutes the first serious, theorised challenge to the 'poetics of oppression' which dominated the drama since the fifth century BCE. But while Epic Theatre rewrites these poetics on many levels, the transformation sought by Brecht remains insufficient because, although the spectator may think and judge the image of the world revealed to her by the play, she has not yet exercised her right to participate in its making. This is the right that Boal has argued for throughout the book and is working to reclaim.

BOAL'S 'POETICS OF THE OPPRESSED'

The two final chapters of *Theatre of the Oppressed* provide an account of Boal's own practice. The first describes the experiments Boal was involved in as part of the Freire-inspired ALFIN project in Peru in 1973. It is this above all for which Boal is famous. The participatory techniques outlined here, of Simultaneous Dramaturgy, Image Theatre, Forum Theatre and others, have been widely adopted by practitioners and are the basis for the subsequent developments of Rainbow of Desire and Legislative Theatre. The content of the second chapter has made less impact. In it Boal sketches the four-phase history of the Arena Theatre in São Paulo from the mid-1950s up to 1966 and argues for the necessity of a *Coringa* (Joker) system, proposed as the company's solution to the challenge of creating a revolutionary theatrical aesthetic. Their aim was clear: to devise a form of theatre that could incorporate both 'the play and its analysis' (1979: 174). The method by which this was to be achieved was considerably more complicated. All *Coringa* plays were to follow a seven-part structure of dedication, explanation, episode, scene, commentary, interview and exhortation, with the 'single perspective' of the 'omniscient' Joker serving to mediate and explicate the diversity of theatrical style and thematic content (1979: 177–84). Only once, in the relatively unsuccessful *Arena Conta Tiradentes*, was the proposal fully adopted. It seems unlikely that so elaborate a system would have lasted much longer, even had the coup of 1968 not forcibly restricted the activities of the 'theatre class' (Boal 2001: 266). Elements of the Joker figure proposed here do find their way into the Joker of Forum Theatre, developed later – crucially, that she is a 'contemporary and neighbour of the spectator' rather than a narrator belonging principally to the world of the play (1979: 175). But at this point in his theatrical evolution Boal still seems some way off from the insistence, repeatedly made in *Theatre of the Oppressed*, that for a truly radical practice the people themselves must take control of the means of theatrical production.

The model for this desired transference of power is inscribed in Boal's account of his work with ALFIN. The intention of ALFIN's theatrical component – in line with the philosophy of the whole – was not to teach participants about theatre as an art form but rather to make it available as a language that could be used by them to address their own needs. With this in mind, the programme did not begin by inviting the group to examine 'finished' examples of theatre, since according to Boal's argument this would have proved alienating rather than inclusive or liberating. Indeed, in the opening stages of the work theatre is hardly mentioned at all. Through a series of simple exercises participants rediscover their own bodies, each person exploring 'its limitations and possibilities, its social distortions and possibilities of rehabilitation' (1979: 126). The methods are manageable by all at each one's level of ability: participants explore different ways to move through space, ways of breathing, ways to give and take weight in interaction with one another, and ways of losing then regaining balance. This kind of journey towards heightened physical awareness via defamiliarisation of the body and a rediscovering of its true capacities will be familiar to any trainee actor, but what is distinct here is the ideological analysis which is never far away from Boal's practice:

> The exercises [. . .] are designed to 'undo' the muscular structure of the participants. That is, to take them apart, to study and analyse them. Not to weaken or destroy them, but to raise them to the level of consciousness. So that each worker, each peasant understands, sees, and feels to what point his body is governed by his work.
>
> (1979: 128)

This process of self-knowing continues into the next stage, in which exercises become increasingly playful. Elements of interpretation and representation are brought in, not of dramatic characters as such, but in the form of children's games and simple rituals. As before, the aim is to recognise one's habitual patterns and find a broader range of possibilities, since individual and social transformation – the ultimate aim – can only be achieved by moving beyond that which is already known and practised.

The third and fourth parts of the programme involve participation in more obviously theatrical activities, but here too the strategy is to provide flexible structures which can be readily adapted by the group, rather than impose existing aesthetic models. These structures involve different degrees and varieties of participation. In Simultaneous Dramaturgy the spectators call out suggestions for action which are immediately improvised by those performing. In Forum Theatre the spectators enact their own suggestions, entering the scenario directly and taking over the role of protagonist. In Image Theatre everyone takes part physically in the exploration of an agreed theme – exploitation, unemployment, oppressions within the family – revealing the diverse meanings it holds for them through 'sculptures' made with their own and each other's bodies (1979: 132–42). Each of these methods adopts a structure or subject that is familiar to the group and applies to this the unknown quantity of improvisation. In this way, Boal argues, the action 'ceases to be presented in a deterministic manner, as something inevitable, as Fate. [. . .] Everything is subject to criticism, to rectification' (1979: 134). The continual emphasis upon multiple interpretations, and on unmaking and remaking, indicates the radical potential of the process. But, for Boal, what is equally important is *who it is* practising it: at last, society's poorest and most disadvantaged – the undifferentiated crowd or comic dupes of the established theatre, if they feature at all – are asserting their right to be authors and actors.

Boal's description of the work in Peru is enormously inspiring, and the techniques outlined here have subsequently been widely adopted – and adapted – by others engaged in similar practices. However, some critics remain unconvinced that Boal provides the evidence to support the claims made for these methods' efficacy. As we have seen, *Theatre of the Oppressed* has persistently argued against a dramatic tradition that, it is suggested, encourages catharsis, harmony and passivity. Boal famously asserts that by contrast the poetics of the oppressed is, if not revolutionary in itself, 'without a doubt a *rehearsal of revolution*'; its forms produce in the spect-actor not the relief of catharsis but 'a sort of uneasy sense of incompleteness that seeks fulfilment through real action' (1979: 141–2). Is this true in practice? If it is, why should this be so? We might accept that the actively participatory process involved, which values and makes space for a sharing of the knowledge individuals already possess, implies a form of learning which is more empowering than obviously didactic methods. But it does not follow from this that learning which takes place in a theatrical context will necessarily be applied beyond it. Milling and Ley are uncertain whether Freire's pedagogic principles of acquiring language skills can be so straightforwardly equated with theatre (2001: 169–70). Increased confidence in a language, developed within the classroom, may well lead to a greater willingness to practise it outside. But Boal claims that his methods inspire participants to take not simply the language of theatre but the content that they have rehearsed and apply it to the reality of their daily lives. Perhaps this doubt can be addressed by returning to the very argument which Boal has pursued throughout *Theatre of the Oppressed*: that aesthetic forms are not neutral vessels to be filled with whatever content one chooses but are themselves politically charged: 'no mere quirk on the part of the individual artist' but 'historically determined by the kind of "content" they have to embody' (Eagleton 1976: 22). From this perspective the poetics of the oppressed *can* be considered 'revolutionary', since it breaks down and transforms the dominant theatrical language, and collapses the invisible fourth wall that has historically divided actor from spectator. If it is true that what has been rehearsed in the context of the group 'seeks fulfilment through real action', this will be so not simply because participants have had the opportunity to practise ways of organising a strike, or of standing up to their employers or family members, but because the theatrical methods in themselves stimulate an appetite for debate, interaction and critical transformation which will not easily be suppressed.

Further questions could be raised about the politics of Boal's work. Can theatre really play a role in social change? Boal's answer is yes, because historically this is just what it *has* done – but it has reinforced systems that have been hierarchical and controlling rather than democratic. Boal began his book by arguing that all theatre is political. If this principle is accepted, then it follows that theatre cannot help but play a part in shaping society; the question is simply how consciously and to what ends you use it. However, you might take the view that theatre's impact can only ever be minimal in relation to the wider scheme of things. This could be true, but it is worth thinking about the heavy censorship the theatre has recurrently experienced under repressive regimes, not only in Brazil: if playwrights, directors and actors are politically ineffectual, why gag them? This is not to say that radical theatre typically provokes spectators/participants to revolt on the streets; it clearly doesn't. Adrian Jackson comments on his own experience of this practice:

> Ultimately the changes that might result are multiple and various, ranging from the world-shattering to the microscopic; but some days nothing might happen. That is reality – change is slow, affected by all sorts of tiny indeterminable unquantifiable factors. It is not that likely, let's face it, that two hours of Forum Theatre is going to reverse a lifetime of homeless abuse and self-abuse – but it might have an influence, and yes, actually, occasionally, miraculously, some-times, it might be the thing that tips that balance [. . .].
>
> (Emailed comments, 6 July 2003)

The work Jackson describes is inspired by the far-reaching ambitions voiced in *Theatre of the Oppressed* – but, as his words imply, it would be unrealistic to evaluate the achievements of day-to-day practice in those terms.

Given how diversely Boal's techniques are practised today – used everywhere from management and business contexts, to therapy sessions – is it still possible to say that this is theatre of the 'oppressed'? As discussed in Chapter 1, some have criticised the psychologically based Rainbow of Desire techniques, particularly seeing in this the virtual abandonment of a broader political agenda (George 1995: 45). The global expansion of Theatre of the Oppressed has created a situa-tion whereby participants in sessions are no longer the socially disenfranchised but are relatively privileged – and as Fortier comments, 'if everyone is oppressed, the category loses its meaning, or at least its political import' (1997: 143). Davis and O'Sullivan are concerned that the techniques frequently encourage individualistic responses that are insufficiently analysed from a class perspective. The tendency of Forum Theatre, they suggest, is to stimulate feelings of self-empowerment in those participants who make seemingly effective interventions, but for

these to remain at the level of transitory and largely personal experience. They argue that Boal's work thus materially diverges from
Freire's principles, since for the latter liberation is only meaningful
when it becomes 'a social act' (2000: 293). But Boal is very clear that
individual experiences of oppression and attempts to fight back *should*
be examined beyond their immediate context. As he states, the Theatre
of the Oppressed ought always to proceed 'from the *phenomenon* toward
the *law*' (1979: 150). In a session of Forum Theatre, for instance, the
combination of a prepared scenario, multiple spectator interventions and collective discussion will ideally result in a shared analysis
of the issue at stake which connects the personal with the general and
thus reveals – rather than reduces – the complexity of the problem.
Certainly, this is not always realised in practice. The problem may lie
in an ill-considered Forum piece, which fails to inspire the range and
quantity of responses necessary for a truly rich debate. It may be that
the actors who have devised it are overly controlling, too certain in
their own minds of what they want spectator interventions to achieve,
over-simplifying the whole enterprise in their determination that the
event 'succeed'. Additionally, and perhaps paradoxically, interventions
might occur whose theatrical impact obscures the question of their
social use-value. The most impassioned, comical or even violent impro-
visations tend to be well received *as performance*, with an audience
correspondingly reluctant or unable to evaluate their strategic potential beyond this. This is a tension at the very heart of Theatre of the
Oppressed: the passion, empathic association and immediacy of participation on which the techniques rely can result in diminution of the
critical awareness or distance needed to process the results.

Chapters 3 and 4 of this book explore these and other questions in
the more telling context of practical application. This chapter has shown
how Boal's poetics were originally framed in theoretical terms, not as
an alternative to the practices of the dominant established theatre but
as a fundamental and necessary unmaking of these in a process of
(re)claiming cultural and political power. *Theatre of the Oppressed*
makes an impassioned case against theatre that serves the interests and
reflects the worldview of the socially privileged. It is true that at times
Boal's historical grand narrative elides complexities and obscures differences. Yet perhaps this is necessary. If Boal's critique were less
absolute, his manifesto would not achieve its extraordinary force of
impact. As Luzuriaga observes, 'many find in the clear-cut nature

of [Boal's] concepts the source of their great influence on so many theatre groups' (1990: 55). *Theatre of the Oppressed* demands change and shows a way in which this might be achieved – even if this is not, in the end, the *only* way. John Arden was right to describe it as a book which everyone engaged in political theatre would do well to read: for vision, scope, commitment, vitality and pragmatism, it would be difficult to find its equal.

3

FORUM THEATRE IN PRODUCTION

As we have seen, productions are not the be-all and end-all of Theatre of the Oppressed but only one possible outcome of an exploratory process. Moreover, those that are created are constantly changing and open to change. This is more than a matter of staying alive and fresh — a quality of all good theatre. A Theatre of the Oppressed production is essentially a starting point, a proposition an audience is invited to contest. In this work, writes Boal, 'we desecrate the stage, that altar over which usually the artist presides alone. We destroy the work offered by the artists in order to construct a new work out of it, together' (Boal 1995: 7). From this perspective the production is the whole event, encompassing both planned and unplanned elements. Could any one production, with one audience, perfectly illustrate Boal's theories in practice? Probably not, since at the heart of the work is the ambition of far-reaching social transformation; no individual event, however well conceived, executed and effectively provocative, could realise this. Furthermore, while one audience might be livelier and more responsive than another, a performance that is slower, its spect-actors reluctant or resentful, can be equally revealing about the nature of the oppression being addressed. For all these reasons this chapter focuses principally on the method of Forum Theatre, using two productions for illustration.

Did Boal invent Forum? He is regularly credited with having done so, but it is possible to find related practices elsewhere. The British Theatre in Education (TIE) movement is one such area. While some TIE companies have made self-conscious use of Theatre of the Oppressed techniques since encountering the work in the 1980s, others used methods akin to Forum Theatre years earlier. The ambitions of Theatre of the Oppressed and TIE are similar: both aim to activate their audiences, creating structures that will facilitate spectators' participation within the drama as makers of meaning and agents of change. Comparison can also be made between Forum Theatre and the 'Conflict Theatre' of Jacob Moreno, creator of psychodrama and group psychotherapy. Moreno identified a four-stage process towards a fully therapeutic theatre: Dogmatic Theatre (the conventional tradition within which the audience remains passive); Conflict Theatre (which combines the actors' play with audience intervention); Theatre of Spontaneity (here theme, plot and development of the piece are agreed collectively and there are no 'spectators'); and Therapeutic Theatre (a cathartic 'theatre of the private sphere', focused on traumatic life moments of participants). As Feldhendler observes, Conflict Theatre corresponds closely to Forum Theatre (just as Therapeutic Theatre resembles Boal's Rainbow of Desire techniques): both forms begin with conventional divisions between actor and spectator, stage and auditorium, and then disrupt these by making space for personal responses and physical intervention (1994: 90–3). The point of these comparisons is not to imply lack of originality on Boal's part but to place Forum Theatre within a wider context. Boal arrived at the method as the next logical step beyond the purely oral participation offered by Simultaneous Dramaturgy. Other practitioners follow different routes, but find the combination of observation and participation, action and discussion, production and process, similarly suited to their needs.

Forum Theatre is probably the most well known and widely practised of all Theatre of the Oppressed techniques. Its popularity might partly be explained by the superficial resemblance it bears to aspects of more conventional forms of theatre. Forum Theatre moves from the familiar to the unfamiliar. Whereas the process-based techniques of Image Theatre or Rainbow of Desire require a commitment to participation from the outset, Forum Theatre initially allows audiences the security of distance and then invites, inspires or provokes them to abandon this in favour of full involvement in the 'theatrical game'

(Jackson, in Boal 1992: xxi). Forum is competitive in that it presents its audience with the challenge of an unsolved problem; one that will matter to them since it impacts on their own lives, directly or indirectly. Its principles are simple. The play – or 'anti-model', as it is sometimes termed – is performed once, so the audience can observe the oppression it illustrates in action, and then repeated. On the second showing, the play will follow the same course until interrupted by a member of the audience, who takes over the role of the protagonist and attempts to redirect the action and ultimately to defeat the oppressors. The rules are explained by the Joker (facilitator), whose function is to invite interventions, assist the transition from spectator to spect-actor, and encourage the audience as a whole to assess the action unfolding before them. The evaluative process is continuous, for rather than any single intervention being judged ideal by the audience the tendency in practice is for one proposed strategy to suggest others, allowing a multitude of ideas to emerge; a range of tactics tested out at different points in the original scenario. Forum Theatre is playfully combative: the spect-actors, taking the part of the oppressed protagonist – literally or metaphorically – pit themselves against the actors playing the oppressors. The former work together, experimenting with all possible manoeuvres to break the pattern of oppression that the Forum play has dramatised, evaluating the success of each in turn, and adding modifications. The latter tend to operate more as individuals, their inventiveness tested as they improvise responses to whatever the spect-actors throw at them, doing all they credibly can to maintain their own power. These elements of unpredictability and creativity make Forum Theatre at its best highly entertaining and challenging, as Adrian Jackson comments giving rise 'to many different kinds of hilarity – laughter of recognition at the tricks of the oppressors, laughter at the ingenuity of spect-actors' ruses, triumphant laughter at the defeat of oppression' (Boal 1992: xxii). At the same time, spontaneous and playful developments occur within a clearly established and essentially simple structure that should ensure that the process – overseen by a careful Joker – remains understandable and accessible to all.

Many questions can be asked about Forum Theatre. For example, should the initial play be simple or complex? Are all interventions valuable, regardless of content? Has the Forum fallen short of its ambitions if some spectators will not participate? Boal examines these and other issues in his useful essay 'Forum Theatre: Doubts and Certainties'

(1992: 224–47) and I address them here through a discussion of specific examples of Forum Theatre in practice. While many instances of Boal's own Forum work are documented in *Theatre of the Oppressed* and *Games for Actors and Non-Actors* these are often somewhat briefly outlined and rarely give information about the process which might have led up to or succeeded the Forum itself. I have chosen instead to focus upon two pieces created by two companies based in the UK, and in what follows I examine in detail both Forum as event and the place of this event within the companies' wider programmes. Names of spect-actors have been changed to preserve anonymity.

CASE STUDIES

CARDBOARD CITIZENS: *GOING . . . GOING . . . GONE . . .*

COMPANY BACKGROUND

Cardboard Citizens is a London-based theatre company, the majority of whose work is directed to audiences of homeless and ex-homeless people, and deals with issues immediately relevant to those audiences. (They are the only professional company in the UK who do this.) The performing company members have all experienced homelessness at some time in their lives, a factor which goes some way towards bridging the distance between the actors and their audiences – a distance likely to be present in any theatre event to a degree, but which may be more noticeable in a context where the latter are justifiably suspicious that the promised entertainment is simply a means by which yet another group of people will advise them how to solve their 'problems'. Cardboard Citizens was founded in 1991 by Adrian Jackson, at the time associate director of the London Bubble Theatre. The company grew out of an initial venture whereby flyers were distributed around London inviting anyone who was homeless or had experienced homelessness to participate in a series of free workshops. The remit of Cardboard Citizens' activities today is wide: they produce touring theatre productions for, by and with homeless people and more general audiences; provide programmes of training in theatre and related skills; and organise opportunities for employment and education. The company's work thus extends far beyond theatre-making; nevertheless this remains central. They strongly uphold the belief that human beings need creativity, entertainment and communality, aware that such needs will almost always be considered secondary to the need for shelter and basic subsistence, if considered at all. Theatre offers a way to meet these needs and more, and Forum Theatre is the method that has been most persistently practised by the company.

Cardboard Citizens' connection with Boal's work is direct. Jackson is English translator of Boal's more recent books and was instrumental in bringing him over to the UK in the late 1980s. Since then, Cardboard Citizens have hosted Theatre of the Oppressed workshops, lectures and training programmes, with Boal and Jackson frequently sharing the facilitation role. Forum Theatre as a model suits the company well. First and foremost, it necessarily presents a story or stories with which the audience can identify, and does so in an entertaining manner. Second, it directly acknowledges issues of power and powerlessness, but suggests that these dynamics are changeable. Third, it is not didactic but rather founded on the belief that audience members themselves have at least some of the answers to the problems enacted. Fourth, it provokes responses from spectators which may be partially or fully theatrical, or may remain at the level of discussion, but which in any case are interactive and critical of the initial, 'authoritative' narrative. Fifth, this activity is contained within a safe space – a 'rehearsal for reality' in which participants can practise and reflect upon possible strategies for change (Boal 1992: xxi). To see how this operates in prac-tice I focus here on one of Cardboard Citizens' Forum Theatre productions, *Going . . . Going . . . Gone . . .*, presented as part of their 2002–3 Engagement Programme.

THE ENGAGEMENT PROGRAMME

The Engagement Programme is one of Cardboard Citizens' long-term projects, originally created in 1999. The Programme uses the inter-active method of Forum Theatre, seeking to inspire homeless people to make changes in their lives by encouraging them to take up any of the opportunities for training, education, guidance and employment the company promote or provide. The 2002 Programme offered courses in computer skills, 'life skills', multimedia, confidence building, and support with job hunting and preparation for work, as well as contact numbers of employers and agencies; arts workshops range from theatre skills to samba. The actors in the Forum also serve as mentors, prepared for this by means of two weeks' training following the four-week period in which the production itself is created and rehearsed. This means that once each Forum has concluded and the company have presented the range of opportunities on offer to the audience, the actors can spend time talking to people one-to-one, discussing possibilities and arranging appointments. Often these result in follow-up meetings and other forms of assistance, such as accompanying individuals on their first engagements. The mentoring concept is especially important to the Engagement Programme; this is the vital link that attempts to ensure that audience members who express the desire to make positive changes in their lives are supported while services are found that can provide longer-term help. This framework of opportunities and care might help to address the concern that Forum Theatre can only offer temporary, illusory empowerment, encouraging spectators to enact alternatives within a fictional context that will never be transferred to reality. However, the strategies adopted by the company do not imply that they consider that concern to be unfounded. Rather, they acknowledge its legitimacy, recognising that, while the performance itself may have an immediate, galvanising impact, more than this is needed for deeper changes to be effected.

It is clearly not possible to produce conclusive statistics detailing how many people have been reached by the Engagement Programme since its inception, and assess what proportion of these were positively or permanently influenced by it. The company operate an extensive tour schedule. Thirty-five performances of the play *A Ridge Too Far* were presented in hostels, day centres and shelters for the 2001–2 Programme; this resulted in 142 engagements (homeless people who went on to engage with a new opportunity). The 2002–3 figures are similar, with the 32 performances of *Going . . . Going . . . Gone . . .* presented as part of the Programme leading to 114 engagements. Of course these figures are small in relation to all the homeless people in London or the country as a whole, but they are substantial enough to have an impact (especially since the Programme constitutes just one of a series of projects the company organises). Nevertheless, any wider changes that might occur could only do so as the cumulative result of individual decisions and actions. Every performance matters and everybody counts: this remains very apparent whether there are 30, 300 or 3 spectators on any one occasion.

GOING . . . GOING . . . GONE . . .

Cardboard Citizens' *Going . . . Going . . . Gone . . .* is a sequence of three short plays, each dealing with a distinct theme relating to homelessness, presented on a single flexible set, together making up a continuous piece of theatre of about half an hour. Having seen the whole, the audience are invited to vote for the individual play they want to see again, which will be interrogated through Forum. There are three principal actors – in the production I saw, Sharon Kirk, Nick Payne and Freddie Still – assisted by Aelaf Agonafir who takes on smaller roles while simultaneously serving as stage manager. There will also be another member of Cardboard Citizens present to perform the Joker function. The company greet each audience, introduce the actors and their roles, refer to the Engagement Programme and hint at how Forum Theatre works before the performance proper begins.

Going . . . Going . . . Gone . . . presents pressing and self-evidently serious issues in a lively, accessible, cartoon-like style. The production demands a high level of energy and concentration from the actors, which helps build audience interest and enjoyment. There are repeated role changes, signalled by the use of selective props or items of costume which complement the actors' physical and vocal characterisations, and the cast frequently rearrange the screens – painted to suggest walls of a room – and blocks that constitute the set. The performance is framed by the metaphor of an auction, implying that the lives of the homeless are disposable or, alternatively, that these are people who are treated as objects rather than human beings. Additionally the pressure of an auction suggests that, for those whose lives are dramatised here, time is running out; if anyone wants to intervene they must do so quickly. The prologue to the performance, shared between the actors, runs as follows:

> What is a life worth?
> Three lives, three stories
> What am I bid? Going, going, gone
> True stories, difficult lives
> Anyone interested?
> The first story, the story of a man in a hostel – Going quietly off his
>   head?
> The second story, the story of someone trying to start over, in their own
>   flat – Going off the rails?

The third story, the story of a woman on the street, and she thinks she's
    stuck there – too far gone?
Going, going – gone (*Auctioneer hits block with hammer*)

This poses a challenge to the audience. These stories are ones which
the spectators know already, or if not these then others which are
similar. These lives are their own lives, or those of friends or people
they've encountered. What are they worth, not simply in the eyes of
'society', but in their *own* eyes? How much are they prepared to risk
to change their own situation? The emphasis is implicitly shifted away
from outsiders who may or may not care about homelessness as an
'issue', to the attitudes of homeless people themselves. From this
opening, the actors begin the first short play.

'Going Quietly Off His Head?'

Payne plays Brian, a man who has recently moved off the streets and
into a hostel. His keyworker, Tony (Still), gives him a lightning tour
of his new home, pointing out the lounge, the office where he can be
found at any time 'but not between five and seven, when we're doing
the handover', and finally Brian's own room, where Tony reels off a
list of 'dos and don'ts' – which are all 'don'ts'. But at least now he has
a room of his own: 'He should be happy – shouldn't he?'.

However grateful Brian might be for shelter, he is painfully lonely
and isolated. He rings old friends, but finds that one's number has been
changed, and another is going on holiday and too busy to see him; life
has moved on. He heads out to buy a bottle of whisky with money
borrowed from loan shark Lush (Kirk), then takes it to his room
ignoring shouts from Lush whose demands had included a share. Once
alone, Brian hears nagging voices in his head (Still and Kirk, wearing
devil's horns). He finds Tony, but is summarily dismissed since it is
'handover' time. Brian's need to talk to someone becomes urgent. He
arranges to meet a friend from the streets, but the latter is too drugged
up to listen. In desperation Brian enters a hospital where he is regarded
with suspicion and quizzed about his drinking. He tries to explain about
the voices, and the feeling that his room is pressing in on him, but is
referred to an addiction clinic.

Something snaps. Brian pours the remains of the whisky around his
bedroom and strikes a match, then watches the blaze from the street.

He demands attention from a policeman: 'I started the fire.' Immediately the scene shifts to an interview room. Brian explains: 'No one would listen to me, so I burned down my flat.' Kirk, as narrator and judge, responds: 'And listen they did, and then a court listened, and a judge listened, everybody was listening now.' Brian is sentenced to five years in prison. He's not alone any more – another man shares his cell.

There follows a musical interlude of perhaps half a minute, in which the actors prepare themselves and the set for the next play:

'Going Off the Rails?' (a version of The Three Little Pigs)

The theme of this play is resettlement and its problems, and, while as serious in subject as the preceding and subsequent plays, it receives a more comic treatment. We are introduced to 'three little homeless piggies', each wearing a snout held on by elastic: Dopey, a blissed-out druggie (Kirk); Psycho, red-faced with permanent rage, and a hammer inside his bomber jacket (Payne); and finally Sensible (Still), the play's optimistic but naive protagonist. The style is close to farce: extreme characterisations, fast pace and comic business as the actors change places, line up, fall over each other. Sensible is the least caricatured; this feels deliberate, since the comedy must not prevent the audience caring about his eventual plight. The mismatched three looked after each other in the hostel, we're told, despite not really being friends. They are bound together by a shared ethos, which initially seems positive: '"We're all in the same boat" . . . "unity in adversity"'.

The first scene shows the three receiving keys to their new homes from the 'resettlement piggy' (Agonafir). Dopey and Psycho grab theirs and go. Sensible is excited about his new-found freedom, and unworried by the resettlement piggy's comment that, although he will try to visit within six months, his heavy workload may delay this longer. The screens and blocks are quickly shifted to represent three flats, side by side. Dopey, says the narrator (Agonafir), built his new life 'on a foundation of grass': we see him happily drawing on a spliff. Psycho – who emerges from behind a screen emptying a handbag and pocketing the money – builds his 'on a foundation of sticks': he brandishes the hammer. By contrast, Sensible follows the approved path: on the government's 'New Deal', he has got himself a job on a deli counter. He is content – if a little lonely.

Problems quickly develop for Dopey. As in the fairy tale, he is visited by a wolf (Agonafir), here 'Mr Wolf, from the Utilities Company', who has a court warrant to disconnect Dopey's trough for non-payment of bills. Dopey resists, but Wolf 'huffs and puffs' and 'blows the house down'. The change to the set is swift and graphic: the walls of the flat are pulled away, and Dopey is left clutching his 'trough' – the wooden block that symbolises the entirety of his possessions. He begs for shelter from Psycho, finally buying his way in with 'uppers, downers and [. . .] Es'. Psycho's 'sty' now has two troughs in it. A comic mime shows what life with Dopey is like: a haze of drugs and drink, funded by the thefts and muggings that Psycho is more than ready to carry out. It is not long before the two are visited by Detective Sergeant Wolf (Agonafir again), since the police believe the premises are being used for illegal activities. As before, he blows the house down. Now there are two homeless piggies and only one place they can think to go.

When Dopey and Psycho turn up at Sensible's flat they give him little option, playing heavily on the 'All for one and one for all' ethos of the hostel inmates. Against his instincts, Sensible lets them in; after all, he has missed companionship. The play hastens to its climax. Predictably, Dopey and Psycho take advantage of Sensible's generosity. He works to support all three of them, while the others lounge around drinking, smoking and failing to pay the rent. They also 'forget' to mention to their host that a housing association representative, concerned about the rent and suspecting multiple occupancy, has visited once already. All three are at home when Dennis Wolf the bailiff (Agonafir, in a third guise) turns up. Dopey and Psycho forcibly prevent Sensible answering the door and set up a barricade. As in the fairy tale, this time the Wolf can't blow the house down so tries instead to come down the chimney. Psycho lights a fire – 'Anyone fancy roasted wolf?' – and the bailiff descends amidst audience laughter, abruptly cut off when Agonafir as narrator remarks in matter-of-fact tone that he 'suffered third degree burns to his whole body, and never worked as a bailiff again' and for the last time lets out the wolf's howl which has punctuated the play: 'Aaaaawwoooooo!'. Dopey and Psycho get five to seven years for GBH; Sensible gets four, for aiding and abetting.

'Too Far Gone?'

The third and final play is possibly the bleakest, perhaps because its main protagonist is barely an adult yet has so little hope. Kirk plays Jennifer, a nineteen-year-old drug addict and prostitute living on the streets. The first image sees her standing on a block centre stage, approaching passing men: 'You looking for business, darling? . . . Do you want business, love?'. Things are alright, she insists; *we* needn't interfere, because *she's* not bothered. But it hasn't always been this way. To the tinkling sound of a music box Jennifer turns, and as she does so the actors remove her jacket and rucksack, wind a grey school uniform skirt around her waist and put an orange baseball cap on her head (see Figure 3.1). She is transformed into a cheerful child in a 'normal' home, with a loving mother (played by Nick Payne, to the amusement of spectators) who buys her whatever she wants, and a father (Agonafir) who may or may not love her but is too busy with his mysterious 'business' to pay her any attention. The audience realises he is dealing dope when Jennifer is discovered selling squares of chocolate to other schoolchildren:

> TEACHER (STILL): Why do you do that, Jennifer?
>
> JENNIFER: That's what my Daddy does, he gets a big bar of stuff and he cuts it into little squares and he wraps it tight in clingfilm.
>
> TEACHER: And then?
>
> JENNIFER: I don't know – I think he gives them to people.
>
> NARRATOR: The teacher didn't get it. And nothing was said, and nothing was done.

Then Jennifer's father disappears – just like that. She begins playing truant from school. At night she hears men's voices along with her mother's from below, and strange sounds whose significance she doesn't understand until another child taunts her for having a mum 'on the game'. After an angry confrontation (see Figure 3.2), Jennifer – age thirteen – runs away. A pattern develops, as she is caught and put in a home, runs again, and is caught again (signalled by forcing her onto stage blocks, one by one). But time passes; now she is sixteen, an adult in her own eyes, at least. She has a boyfriend (Agonafir) who she says takes care of her, but seemingly serves as her pimp; he pockets her money, promising to 'sort her out later' with heroin. We see how one thing leads to, or depends on, another: prostitution provides money;

Figure 3.1 Teacher comments on Jennifer's progress, in Cardboard Citizens' *Going . . . Going . . . Gone . . . .* Photograph by Dee Conway

Figure 3.2   Jennifer confronts her mother. Photograph by Dee Conway

money provides drugs. She must look good to attract punters, so that requires shoplifting or other small thefts. We see only one attempt by someone to help her break this cycle. Gordon, a care worker (Agonafir) tries talking to her. Wouldn't she like to change? Take a course, maybe? She ridicules his offers, snapping viciously: 'I've never had anyone's help in all my life, piss off and leave me be!'.

The situation worsens. Jennifer's drug habit intensifies and health deteriorates, which makes it both harder and simultaneously more imperative that she find punters. In the play's final scene we see a man (Still) persuading her to bend her rules and give him 'sex without a condom, for £10 and a rock'. She wants to refuse, but weakens – and the play ends with the narrator asking: 'Does she say yes, or does she say no? [. . .] Should she say yes, or could she say no?'. Leaving this hanging in the air, the play concludes by repeating the invitation with which it began:

STILL: Three stories, three lives
          What am I bid?

What's a life worth?

Going . . . Going . . .

ALL: Gone.

THE PLAY AS FORUM

Going . . . Going . . . Gone . . . is short – each narrative approximately ten minutes long – but densely structured. The questions it raises are clear. How could Brian have made himself heard sooner, and less violently? How could Sensible have resisted the insistence of his 'friends' and kept his flat? The third play invites us to look forward, as well as back: can anything improve for Jennifer? It takes considerable skill to reveal problems so starkly, in a manner that entertains yet avoids reductiveness. Theatrical stylisation assists this: it keeps us engaged as an audience because we admire the cast's ingenuity and dexterity; it allows the narrative to shift location and across time, and thus indicates the development and impact of damaging actions on perpetrators and those around them; yet for all this, it is not so extreme as to be alienating. Each play incorporates likely moments when intervention can occur, and others that are less obvious. The focus of Forum is always – at least initially – on how the protagonist herself could effect change, rather than how other characters might offer help. What could these three have done differently? In order to examine how *Going . . . Going . . . Gone . . .* works as Forum, I will discuss its reception in two contexts: with young residents at a YMCA and with the adult residents of a hostel.

Earls Court YMCA, West Cromwell Road, Earls Court (2 December 2002)

Earls Court YMCA provides accommodation for about thirty young people (ages sixteen to twenty-five). The average length of stay is six months, though in some cases it is as short as a few weeks or as long as a year. Ideally residents depart because they are moving into housing or a longer-stay hostel, but on occasion they will be asked to leave because of 'anti-social' behaviour, or may simply remove themselves and disappear from the system.

Going . . . Going . . . Gone . . . was performed in a basement room, normally used by the residents for playing pool. The space would have been small even if the pool table were removed altogether, but instead it was pushed into the bay window and covered with props and costumes. The modest set almost filled the room, leaving room for only about twelve chairs. As it turned out, this was plenty. At the time the performance was due to start the only spectators – other than me – were two hostel staff, and it seemed likely that the company would cancel. But then three lads appeared, which decided it. Dave, the most talkative of the three, announced that someone else was definitely coming: Julie would 'be down in a bit'. They should not wait, he added, since he himself had to leave in twenty minutes' time. The company were uncertain, knowing that the play on its own lasts half an hour, Forum aside, and if one spectator leaves early the others may be less inclined to stay or participate. Tony McBride, as Joker, proposed they do just one of the playlets, but Dave would not accept the compromise. The company should hurry up and start, and do what they normally do; despite his own unwillingness to offer more than a partial attendance, he would not hear of them presenting a partial performance. At this point Julie arrived, and in the buzz around her entrance the company decided to go ahead with the piece as usual. There was a brief false start when Dave's mobile phone rang during McBride's introduction and he took the call unperturbed, but after this there were no further interruptions.

The performance was positively received by the tiny audience, with appreciative laughter and frequent comments throughout. At seven o'clock the actors were about halfway through, and although this was the time Dave had to 'be somewhere' he didn't move, despite nudgings from his friend. In fact he stayed for the whole performance, as did they all. The play over, the audience applauded and made moves to go but were halted by McBride who asked them to stay for 'just a couple of minutes'. They did – and two minutes became five, then ten, then twenty, as they were drawn into participation almost without realising it. McBride skilfully handled the Joker's role: 'I know you have to leave in a minute, but which story would you choose to look at if you *did* have time?'. They agreed it would be Jennifer's story – significantly, the one with the youngest protagonist. 'What we would normally do, if you had time, would be to ask what you thought were Jennifer's problems. Out of interest, what do you think they were?'. The answers came readily enough. Jennifer's troubles began in her family: her parents' separation was one factor, and the lack of a positive role model was seen as another. Jennifer's boyfriend was a problem, suggested Julie, since he was effectively her pimp. Kirk chipped in from where she was sitting, in character: 'But he takes care of me – I love him!', to which Julie retorted: 'You love him, but he's bad for you.'

McBride pushed the discussion further, using the same tactics to forestall the young people's departure. 'Normally we'd see if you thought it was possible to change anything – do you think it is? And if there was one scene you'd choose where things could be changed, which would it be?'. They agreed on an early moment when Jennifer still lived at home, not so far back that everything was good, but nevertheless before problems have really developed. This is hard to pinpoint, but eventually they settled on the image of Jennifer sitting on the sofa watching television with her mother, immediately after her father's disappearance. The actors set it up. Some of the usual rituals of Forum were bypassed in this process. It was more a still image than a scene, and no one called 'stop' – McBride simply asked the audience whether Jennifer could do anything to improve things. There was some hesitation; although not articulated directly, the spectators clearly understood that Jennifer's serious problems – prostitution and addiction – had not yet emerged and that they couldn't reasonably anticipate this later development from the evidence before them. Julie proposed that Jennifer try talking to her mother properly, confronting the situation rather than avoiding it and cosily watching television. She was invited to enter the scene and replace Jennifer, which perhaps surprisingly she did immediately. But once 'onstage', even though this was only three steps from her chair, she lost confidence – 'I don't know what to do, what am I supposed to say – I can't believe I'm doing this' – but regained it when Dave got up to go; she told him smartly to sit back down, and he did. Julie tried to play the scene but seemed nervous about 'acting' and instantly froze, yet this was seized on by McBride as an opportunity to draw other spectators in to assist. This worked wonderfully. When Julie, as Jennifer, said to her mother that she wanted them to do things together, as a family, Dave instructed her to take away her mother's magazine: 'She's not really listening to you!'. Julie twitched it from Payne's grasp, and tried again. Another comment came from the audience: 'She's still looking at the telly . . .'. Julie turned Payne's head towards her: 'Mum, *look at me* when I'm talking to you!'.

In the event, this was the extent of the Forum process. But despite its brevity the perceptiveness shown by the spectators was startling. They had not chosen an obviously dramatic scene. They recognised instead that an interpersonal dynamic could be subtly shifted by addressing small details, and that the changes were worth making since they could alter the course of someone's life. The tiny audience worked collectively: Julie was their representative onstage, but the strategies she adopted were proposed by the group. And around three-quarters of an hour after he 'had' to have left, Dave was still there, taking a leading role in discussion. It seemed he enjoyed the performance too much to leave before seeing how it concluded, and once lured into the debate he couldn't bear not to have his say. He still stayed, half in the doorway and half out, while McBride outlined the Engagement Programme and the kinds of opportunities that could be taken up. He showed some interest, took a leaflet and at last made his exit, though not before he had shaken everybody's hand and kissed Kirk on both cheeks. After this, the atmosphere quieted. The other residents read the company's cards and leaflets while the actors dismantled the set (two minutes) and then, almost invisibly, the mentoring process began. Suddenly the advantages of such a small audience were obvious; actors and spect-actors chatted one-to-one, with nobody waiting around or, equally likely, slipping away without returning. Obviously, these discussions were private, but it was evident that their individual situations and desires varied significantly. One wanted a job (any job); another wanted to be apprenticed to a decorator; a third thought he might try out a theatre or singing workshop. All pairs made follow up arrangements: exchanging phone numbers, agreeing times to call, making dates to meet for coffee. The actors' friendliness and evident familiarity with the kind of situations the young people had to deal with were clearly crucial to the success of the contact.

St Martin of Tours Hostel, New North Road, Islington (10 December 2002)

St Martin of Tours is a long-stay hostel providing accommodation for adult men with mental health problems, the majority of whom are ex-offenders. Cardboard Citizens performed in the lounge-cum-pool room, a larger space than that used in Earls Court, but equally informal. There was an audience of about twelve men, ranging in age from twenties to perhaps late fifties, plus two hostel workers. The atmosphere before the actors began was muted; the audience hardly spoke to each other but just sat, waiting. Some, perhaps, were not even doing that; they were sitting in their lounge, as they would do normally, as if the company were not there. Adrian Jackson was the Joker, and in the generous pause the company allow to see if anyone else will appear he moved around the room chatting to residents: asking names, how long people have been there, what they thought of the hostel. He maintained this gentle, low-key style in the official welcome and introduction, leaving it to the actors to provide the upbeat energy and provocation in the show itself.

It is not easy to judge what the St Martins residents thought of *Going . . . Going . . . Gone.* . . . They were quiet, largely attentive, seemingly less amused than the YMCA audience (perhaps more pessimistic). They were certainly passive, at least initially; when Jackson tried to begin the discussion he had to work hard to draw out any reactions at all. But then one man – Richard – started talking, and once one had said something a couple of others were prepared to, but as it turned out Richard was so articulate it was hard for anyone else to get a word in edgeways. All in all, it took a good twenty minutes of questioning, jokes and other stratagems to arrive at a point when the audience had voted – after a fashion – for the third narrative: Jennifer's story.

'Gone Too Far?' was replayed from the beginning. The action was stopped simultaneously by Richard and another resident, Matthew, at the point when Jennifer is discovered selling chocolate. Both were concerned, not so much by Jennifer's behaviour, as by the teacher's failure to recognise its significance; there was agreement that he 'should have done something'. Jackson asked how the teacher ought to have behaved. It was clearly too soon to expect either of them to enter the performance space – and Richard, anyway, was adamant he would not act – so Kirk, as Jennifer, simply came into the audience. Matthew was prepared to adopt the teacher's role from where he sat:

TEACHER (MATTHEW):   Jennifer, why are you doing this?

JENNIFER: It's what my Dad does – and he has loads of mates, so I thought that if I did it, I'd have loads of mates too. . . . Am I in trouble?

TEACHER: No, you're not in trouble. But will you ask your Dad to come in to see me, please?

As sometimes happens in Forum, the focus shifted away from the capabilities of the protagonist towards the responsibilities of other figures within the drama. It is possible to question the validity of this move – as Boal has done elsewhere – on the grounds that turning unhelpful antagonists into caring and attentive supporters is in a sense to offer 'magic' solutions (1992: 239). But the intervention was more complex than this analysis would suggest. We applauded Matthew's transformation of the teacher into a more proactive figure, but recognised that the problem had not been solved. Kirk and Agonafir briefly improvised a scene at home between Jennifer and her father, the former confused but standing her ground, the latter angry about the interference (see Figure 3.3). He gave her reassurances – and money for more sweets – but evidently had no intention of making the appointment. Discussion followed about what would happen next: the father's failure to show up might set alarm bells ringing; alternatively, the opportunity might slip away with Jennifer becoming more secretive about her home life. Boal has stated that 'it is more important to achieve a good debate than a good solution', a view I have doubted in the past but the truth of which now struck me (1992: 230). Matthew's intervention did not in itself 'save' Jennifer but stimulated others to engage with the issue of how she might be saved, or might save herself. He did not replace the protagonist, but did participate. He did not leave his seat, but, since the performance extended to include him where he was, the actor-spectator divide was equally brought into question.

From these small beginnings developed a surprisingly lengthy Forum session. Of all the residents, Matthew was the most willing to engage actively with the performance, and as the evening proceeded he directed all his energies into exploring strategies for change. He was supported by Gerry, a hostel worker, who became very involved once reassured that he was 'allowed' to participate. Richard was most ready to pursue issues through discussion, though at times he struck a bitter, fatalistic note. I was aware that his contributions frequently pulled against those of others, questioning the worth of individual changes and, by implication, of intervention itself. But it remained a 'good debate', since Jackson did not deny Richard's pessimistic vision but simply reflected it back to the rest of the audience: 'Is this how you see the world?'. And if it wasn't, they were the more encouraged to show alternatives.

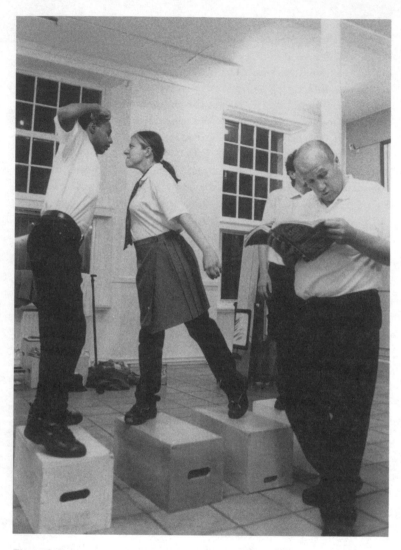

Figure 3.3 Jennifer tells her father she is in trouble at school. Photograph by Dee Conway

The Forum turned to later scenes, where Jennifer h
and is effectively living on the streets. By this point, sev
were talking – and they were unanimous that what Jennif
support, if she was to change anything. Gerry stopped the scene ...
which the care worker offers help but is rebuffed. He took over the
role, participating physically, pulling on Jennifer's backpack as a signi-
fier (the first time 'classic' Forum procedure had been followed). The
scene went very differently, since this Jennifer admitted that she *did*
need help. Discussion broke in immediately. Was this realistic? Would
Jennifer even know the kind of help she needs? They agreed she must
have a mentor, though whether this should be a social worker, doctor
or simply a friend was uncertain. Matthew accepted the role, and this
time came onstage and stayed there, even when Gerry returned to his
seat. A scene was improvised in which Matthew accompanied Jennifer
to meet a social worker. Kirk, as Jennifer, barely spoke, so it was left
to Matthew to take charge – which he did, pressing for increased
commitments for Jennifer's support. As with the Earl's Court Forum,
whenever there was doubt about how to proceed, suggestions were
invited from the floor. The residents knew what Jennifer needed, from
their own experiences: how to avoid relapses; an emergency contact
number; a change of environment; friends, a social life; someone to
help her process feelings about her childhood.

Eventually Jackson had to bring things to a close. One resident asked
for a 'happy ending', and in this hopeful spirit we were asked to imagine
what progress Jennifer might make over the next few years, based on
the changes implied by preceding interventions. We proposed that
Jennifer had completed detox; was sharing a flat with a friend who was
not yet a boyfriend but might become one; he had a job and she was
studying at college with a view to a career in social services. Jackson
asked for suggestions of a future event that could be enacted, and before
anyone else could speak Richard brightly offered 'her mother's funeral'.
We accepted both this and the idea from Paul that Jennifer's father
might be there too. Jennifer's reaction to her Dad, says Paul, should
be 'angry at first, then resigned, then she should give him a hug'. This
was idealistic, in the circumstances, but we were giving ourselves
permission for idealism. The scene was set; Jackson drew in two others,
casting them as mourners with the assurance that they wouldn't have
to speak. Payne played the Vicar, Still the boyfriend-in-waiting. Jackson
inserted additional theatrical touches, giving the mourners a box to

represent a coffin, directing them to make an entrance and help establish the solemn atmosphere; they ended up doing more 'acting' than they had intended, and seemingly enjoyed it. The encounter between Kirk and Agonafir was tense, had few words and felt awkward both emotionally and from an acting viewpoint. They embraced, as instructed, but it was an uncomfortable 'happy ending'; whatever the intention, no escapism was possible here.

A couple of residents disappeared immediately after the Forum but others hung around, looking as if they wanted to be spoken to even if they would not make the first move. While the actors talked with them about the Engagement Programme I overheard Benny, who had watched the event without comment, complimenting Jackson on the work. He remarked that, while plenty of people only know what they've read in books, 'you lot seem to understand what you're talking about', and was regretful about the turn his own life had taken. He had a good job as a security guard, with 'a uniform, the works', but lost it all through a drug habit that became an addiction. 'It wasn't worth it.' Then he laughed, adding: 'but life's not over yet . . .'.

MIND THE GAP AND SFX THEATRE COMPANY: *NEVER AGAIN!*

COMPANY BACKGROUND

Mind the Gap is a professional theatre company of charitable status based in Bradford, dedicated to making work with learning disabled artists. Since 1988, when it was founded by Tim Wheeler and Susan Brown, Mind the Gap has created regular national touring, regional and local productions, both devised and of pre-written texts, alongside an ever-expanding programme of workshops, education and development projects. The company policy derives from a belief in quality, equality and inclusion. They aim to 'dismantle the barriers to artistic excellence so that learning disabled and non-disabled artists can perform alongside each other as equals' (http://www.mind-the-gap.org.uk). Perhaps the most ambitious undertaking of recent years towards this end has been the design and implementation of an accredited theatre-training programme for young adults with a learning disability. Initially a three-year National Lottery-funded apprenticeship titled Making Waves, the scheme has now been relaunched as a condensed one-year programme, Making Theatre, accepting around twelve students per year. Like Cardboard Citizens, Mind the Gap recognises that, if the impact of their work is to be long-term and far-reaching, theatrical practice can only be one strategy among many. Thus students on the programme learn skills in marketing and management as well as performance, and take up placements at local arts and other cultural organisations. A primary aim of Making Waves was realised when in the autumn of 2001 six of its graduates formed their own user-led theatre company, SFX, with Mind the Gap's support.

Mind the Gap has a long association with Boal and his work. Wheeler first encountered him in the late 1980s and Boal has worked directly with the company on several occasions since, most recently in 1999 when he served as guest tutor to the Making Waves apprentices (see Figures 3.4 and 3.5). Theatre of the Oppressed's flexible and inter-active methods have served the company well. Since the company's inception it has produced around twenty Forum Theatre events, and Forum as a devising and performance mode is an integral part of the Making Theatre training programme. The method suits their purposes, since the 'dismantling of barriers' is inherent in its very structure. Additionally, the spirit of playful competition in which Forum ideally operates can prove particularly liberating for participants with learning difficulties. As Ann Cattanach observes, 'much time is spent by those who care in exhorting them to be responsible and sometimes this external pressure to achieve some kind of independence makes people with learning difficulties afraid to play and have fun' (Cattanach 1992: 89). Forum Theatre is one means by which participants can recover their capacity for play and give it expression. But Mind the Gap has also discovered other ways in which Forum can be useful to the company, as demonstrated by its role within their recent audience development project, Incluedo.

INCLUEDO

Incluedo is an action research project designed by Mind the Gap aiming to identify and overcome the barriers which inhibit the involvement of young people – especially young people with a learning disability – in the arts. The company is concerned to facilitate the watching of theatre, as well as direct participation in its creation. However, it is one thing to advocate that the arts should be accessible to all but quite another

Figure 3.4 Augusto Boal, with Mind the Gap. Photograph by Tim Smith

to develop a climate of equality whereby this is truly possible. With Incluedo, a three-year programme launched in 2000 and funded by Yorkshire Arts, Mind the Gap took decisive steps towards achieving this.

The project incorporated five key stages. In Stage One, the company ran a series of workshops with learning-disabled students on the Making Waves Apprenticeship together with non-disabled young people from Bradford, the aim being to explore prevailing attitudes to the arts in general and theatregoing in particular. This led to Stage Two, in which the participants went as undercover agents to three West Yorkshire arts venues, to judge the professional theatre's 'accessibility' first-hand. The data gathered through this process was used by the Making Waves students in Stage Three: the creation of a Forum play, *Never Again!*, presented in schools for disabled and non-disabled audiences (reaching around 250 young people in total at these events). Stage Four was a half-day conference that offered up the project's findings for debate, run by the company and disability access organisation ADA Inc. and attended by arts personnel working in programming, front of house and marketing across the region. An additional, tangible product has just been created in Stage Five: a CD-ROM, designed primarily for use

Figure 3.5 Augusto Boal. Photograph by Tim Smith

by arts organisations as a training resource to help them widen access and hence improve their service.

For *Includo*, Mind the Gap used Forum Theatre both conventionally and unconventionally. The method provided a creative means of sharing and structuring young people's diverse experiences and taking these to a wider audience, which in turn led to further expansions and refinements. The Forum demanded research, as is typical, but additionally the Forum was itself research for a further collective project, the CD-ROM (launched in 2004). The marriage of Forum with CD-ROM technology may be initially surprising, yet is in many ways an appropriate and promising partnership. Both forms readily employ 'graphics' alongside text, frequently discovering that a simple, almost cartoon-like style best suits their needs; evidently both must entertain in order to engage and educate; both set up scenarios / images but allow the user to pursue different pathways through these as they choose. Possibly as yet Forum Theatre allows greater freedoms, but both provide an experience that is interactive rather than essentially a fixed product.

Like Cardboard Citizens, Mind the Gap has chosen to include Forum as a central component of a wider and more ambitious programme.

The Forum process of *Going . . . Going . . . Gone . . .* seeks to stimulate the participation of homeless people in a theatrical debate around issues of immediate relevance to them, and from there to facilitate their engagement with other services. Mind the Gap's *Never Again!* is aimed both at young people – especially those with learning difficulties – and at professional arts providers, and attempts to bridge the two, in conscious recognition that substantial change is most likely to be achieved through collaboration. As In*clue*do's 2001 progress report emphasises, it is now unlawful for organisations not to take 'reasonable steps' to ensure their services can be accessed by those with disabilities. This implies that a Forum Theatre project on this issue can and should go only so far in exploring the means by which the protagonist herself could shake off oppression. Of course this investigation is valuable, in terms both of its effect upon individual participants and for the ideas it might provoke. But the fact that *Never Again!* is incorporated as part of a complex and far-reaching project is an acknowledgement that the problem of exclusion is not one which those who are discriminated against must solve unaided, on the basis of their individual capacity for self-assertion.

NEVER AGAIN!

SFX Theatre Company's *Never Again!* is a fifteen-minute Forum play dramatising the experience of a young adult with a learning disability when she goes to see a performance at a nearby theatre. *Never Again!* opens with a family – mother (Lynn Williams), father (Kevin Pringle), sons (Alan Clay and Neil Heslop) and daughter (Susan Middleton) – sitting around the kitchen table playing Cluedo. The set is simply a table and chairs; the costumes ordinary everyday clothes with the addition of specific items as conventional signifiers: an apron for mother, a newspaper for father. The edges of the acting area are defined by two hat stands draped with coats and other props for later use. A broadly realistic opening sequence is disrupted by the entrance of a second daughter (Anna-Marie Heslop), aged nineteen, who speaks to the audience directly:

> Hello everybody. I'm Anna, and this is my family. As you can see I've got Down's Syndrome, and sometimes people treat me differently. . . .

Anna has a special request. She has been reading the local theatre's brochure and is desperate to go, but needs someone to accompany her. She overrules her mother's initial objection on the grounds of cost, since according to the brochure 'carers go free'. Her mother then vetoes Anna's choice of play, judging *Death of a Salesman* too morbid on the basis of its title and instead recommending *The Phantom of the Opera*. But mother won't go too; father grunts and disappears deeper into his newspaper; brothers are otherwise engaged. This leaves Anna's older sister who gives in grudgingly, making it clear she would rather spend the evening with her boyfriend. Mother gives her £10 for a ticket and strict instructions not to let Anna out of her sight.

Scene two takes place at the theatre's box office (see Figure 3.6). Within a minute the stage is transformed, the table framed in purple velvet, gold fringe and tassels. Anna and her sister are uncertain at first where to find the entrance to the building; there are no clear signs. Once inside, Anna goes up to the booth in some confusion:

ANNA: Excuse me, where do we buy a ticket?
RECEPTIONIST (WILLIAMS):   (*condescendingly*) This is the Box Office.
ANNA: Yes, but where do we buy tickets?
RECEPTIONIST: (*louder, irritated*) This is the Box Office! This is where you buy a ticket!

Anna proceeds with the purchase but runs into difficulties almost immediately, since the receptionist knows nothing about the carers scheme and insists they buy a ticket each. Anna shows her the small print, but she remains obstructive: 'You're not in a wheelchair . . .'. Meanwhile, a queue has built up behind Anna, and there are weary sighs and irritated mutterings. Anna's sister has had enough; giving Anna the £10 note, she departs to find her boyfriend. Anna tries to get a seat near the front since her eyesight is not good, but none are available. Ten pounds can only buy her one where the vision is partially obstructed, but after all, as the receptionist informs her, 'we do recommend that people with special needs book in advance'. As this is Anna's first visit the receptionist asks for her details in order to put her on the mailing list, but since she doesn't explain that this is what she's doing, Anna is further puzzled on being asked her name, address and postcode. 'DO-YOU-KNOW-HOW-TO-SPELL-YOUR-NAME?'. presses the receptionist impatiently, provoking further grumblings

Figure 3.6 The Box Office scene in *Never Again!* by Mind the Gap and SFX.
Photograph by Tim Smith

among those queuing. Anna obligingly provides the required information; within this encounter it seems as if she alone is able to be tolerant
and patient. Clutching her ticket she asks where she should go next but
is dismissed with the injunction to 'Follow the signs!' as the receptionist
turns to greet a comical series of 'important' theatre-goers:

> Ah, Councillor, have you come for your complimentary ticket? Ah, it's Barry
> Normal! Ah, Lord Chumleigh – and Lady Chumleigh! Thank you very very very
> very very much for patronising us. . . .

Anna is left staring up at a signpost with arrows in all different directions, suggesting multiple possibilities but not one telling her straightforwardly what she needs to know (see Figure 3.7).

Suddenly Anna is surrounded by the rest of the cast. She has
wandered into the bar, ignored and talked over by a crowd of noisy
theatregoers elbowing each other out of the way as they demand to be
served. She stands no chance of getting a drink, and visibly panics
on hearing the announcement over the tannoy that the performance
will begin in 'five minutes . . . three minutes . . . one minute . . .',

Figure 3.7 Anna-Marie Heslop in *Never Again!*. Photograph by Tim Smith

still unsure where it will take place. She does find it, but the rest of the spectators are already seated and the show started – 'Latecomers!' mutters one. She asks for help finding her place and in response the usher virtually carries her to it, asking: 'Where's your Mum?'.

Although Anna is now in the theatre and in her proper seat, the difficulties are not over. She cannot see properly, but is reproved by the other spectators when she shifts around to get a better view. She is confused about the action onstage, turns to her neighbour for an explanation but is hushed, asks to borrow her programme and is told sharply to buy her own. When the Phantom appears she boos enthusiastically, and the exasperated spectators call the usher to complain. She is told to leave if she can't be quiet. She protests – 'I've paid to be here like everyone else!' – but is soon driven to depart, distressed: 'That's it – never again!'. The stage audience agrees, echoing her words back to her: 'Never again!'.

There is a small coda to the play. With no one to accompany her and no money left for a bus, Anna nervously walks home alone. She is shaken by her experience at the theatre, and bitter too: 'Mum was right – what a waste of a good ten quid!'. When she finally gets back, an hour and a half later, she finds her mother anxious and cross: 'You could've been murdered! I can't let you out on your own again . . .'.

THE PLAY AS FORUM

Never Again! lasts just fifteen minutes but, like *Going . . . Going . . . Gone . . .*, is tightly constructed to incorporate a range of issues and multiple opportunities for audience intervention. The prior experience and active research of the young people involved in the Incluedo project helped to identify a whole series of 'barriers to inclusion' which are woven into the play. *Never Again!* highlights difficulties around economic access to the arts, drawing attention not only to high ticket prices or inadequate concessionary schemes, but to the additional and often forgotten expense of an accompanying carer. Physical access is another problem, but as the play reveals this is not necessarily overcome by ensuring that ramps, lifts and so on are installed. Anna is confused by the theatre's appearance and layout, and has trouble just locating the entrance; this moment distils the comments of the researchers that performance venues today are as likely to resemble 'museums, swimming pools, car parks and restaurants' as conventional theatre establishments. Once inside the building, information still may not be easily accessible. Theatre staff watching *Never Again!* are provoked into thinking afresh about their own venue: heights of counters, systems of signage, lighting, seat numbers. Third the play considers attitudinal access, and tackles the problem of discriminatory behaviour from arts employees and other spectators. It might be thought that *Never Again!* paints a deliberately negative picture in order to provoke, but on the basis of the Incluedo 'undercover' research it is discouragingly accurate, albeit comically heightened. Young people were 'ignored, patronised and made to feel as if they shouldn't be there', staff were thought 'unsmiling', and one or two visitors with a learning disability had problems being understood and felt that box-office personnel would have preferred to deal with a non-disabled adult rather than with them directly. Williams' receptionist character makes false assumptions about the nature of Anna's disability on the basis of her physical appearance and ignorance of theatregoing conventions, and has not been informed about the scheme her employers have instigated. Both characters are additionally pressured by those others impatiently waiting in the queue, and this question of spectator attitudes is perhaps even more problematic since particularly difficult to tackle. Anna is received with hostility by her neighbours because – in their view – she speaks when she should be quiet, moves when she should be still, cheers and boos when she should adapt her responses to fit a polite, middle-class consensus. It is a provocative sequence and one likely to produce mixed reactions among Forum spectators: who should adapt to whom?

As noted, Incluedo aims to create bridges between arts organisations and new potential audiences. It is recognised that both parties may have to change their past practices to some degree for this to happen. *Never Again!* is evidently designed to draw attention to the limitations within existing arts provision and expose the need for further reform; these are not problems which the protagonist is likely to be able to solve on her own. But it is perhaps unwise to take this line of reasoning too far, since it could mask a position of unconscious patronage. It should not be assumed that people with a learning disability are incapable of standing up for their rights and that this must therefore be done on their behalf. Certainly, any such misapprehension was overturned by seeing *Never Again!* in performance. What follows is an account of the play in Forum with Mind the Gap's own Making Theatre students, and then at a Bradford school when it toured again the following year.

Queen's House, Queen's Road, Bradford (26 November 2002)

When I first saw *Never Again!* performed live, it was at Mind the Gap's own building and in somewhat unusual circumstances. It had already been presented several times in schools and colleges in the Bradford district to audiences of learning-disabled and non-disabled students but on this occasion was being filmed by Yorkshire Television, who were compiling a feature on actress Anna-Marie Heslop for their magazine programme *Same Difference* (broadcast 26 February 2003). Diverse, and potentially conflicting, agendas were in operation: the TV team were focused on Heslop rather than the play as such, whereas the Making Theatre students who formed the audience were concentrating on the Forum, a mode they had not previously encountered but would themselves be studying later that year. Wheeler was uncertain how effectively these ambitions would come together: the cameras might prove inhibiting for the spectators; the crew could have trouble establishing 'continuity' filming an event which, of necessity, would never be the same twice running.

Never Again! was presented to audience of about fifteen, of whom nine were Making Theatre students. There was a good deal of laughter and pretended fear around the presence of cameras and crew, but all things considered they were relatively unfazed. In many respects there was a striking lack of inhibition – a characteristic *Never Again!* directly dramatises in Anna's unselfconscious reactions to the performance she sees. When Wheeler said he was going to introduce Anna, a student responded matter-of-factly: 'I know her already – she's a friend of Ben's.' As with Cardboard Citizens, the aim and rules of Forum were explained as straightforwardly as possible without any references to 'oppressors' or 'protagonists'. It was presented as a kind of game that could be used to help people solve some of their problems. This premise was readily accepted – though the students decided to adopt 'Cut!' rather than 'Stop!' as more appropriate to the occasion – and Heslop stepped forward to outline the history of the In*clue*do project and *Never Again!*'s place within it.

The audience clearly enjoyed the play and appreciated its relevance. The students frequently talked to each other while it was going on, usually to check that they had heard or understood correctly. Elements of direct audience address proved popular although, understandably, these were treated as opportunities to talk back to the actors. (SFX's performers could easily accommodate this since it was to a degree anticipated by them, but with different actors the evident one-sidedness of this convention could be comically exposed.) Afterwards, Wheeler invited the audience to discuss the play in detail. They were encouraged to identify the kinds of problems that Anna encounters and to share suggestions as to how her experience might be improved. As obvious as this procedure might sound, it is not always adopted in Forum. The wish to emphasise active intervention (Boal 1992: 19–21) has led some practitioners to limit or exclude initial discussions, not least because the desire to achieve maximum *theatrical* impact seems to imply that spectators' interventions should ideally come as a complete surprise. But to adhere to this strictly is to underestimate the nature of the challenge Forum can present. In practice, a discussion stage can help build confidence within an audience that they have something to offer and thus stimulate rather than repress the desire for physical participation. In this particular context, it worked to galvanise the spectators into action. One student summarised for the rest: 'Our mission – should we choose to accept it – is to change the course of the play so it doesn't end up the same way, with Mum going ballistic . . .'.

Meanwhile, the cameras had been rearranged in order to re-shoot the play from a different angle. The actors began *Never Again!* a second time, the tension in the audience palpable. After a minute Wheeler interrupted the action himself, to joke: 'Isn't it odd having a film crew in your home?', which eased this a little. The first intervention, from Lucy – one of the more obviously confident students – came in the scene where family members try to push onto each other the responsibility of accompanying Anna to the theatre. Lucy/Anna tried to combat Anna's relative isolation and sense of herself as a burden by suggesting they all go as a family, making it clear how much this would mean to her. But the characters – as always in Forum – were resistant. Williams as mother was a particularly tough customer, insisting that this would be prohibitively expensive and, moreover, Anna's father would undoubtedly fall asleep 'and I don't want to listen to him snoring!'. Wheeler invited the audience to evaluate the intervention. They considered that although not ultimately persuasive it had some effect, if only in making the family members feel guilty; it also inadvertently stimulated a brief and useful discussion about the availability of discounts on group bookings.

No further interventions were made within this scene. The next came during the box office sequence. This new Anna, a tall man squeezed into the diminutive character's duffel coat, adopted an assertive approach. Jack/Anna stood up for herself in the encounter with the receptionist, criticised the latter's unhelpful attitude and eventually asked for the manager. Such a meeting could be improvised, but on this occasion Williams told her flatly that it was impossible as he was away. The actors forming the queue built up the pressure with complaints and pushing, and at this point Anna's sister decided to leave, as in the original. But before she could depart, Lucy leaped up from the audience again and joined her fellow student to make a sort of double Anna: 'Don't go!', she pleaded, 'Don't leave me! I'll let you wear my favourite T-shirt – I'll give it to you!'. There was a lot of laughter at this new strategy, but a degree of disapproval as well: surely Anna shouldn't have to beg? A new spect-actor tried a strategy. Michael/Anna made no attempt to forestall the sister's exit but held her ground and was, quite simply, very insistent on her rights – a tactic that resulted in a standoff with little evident progress for either party. This stalemate was only broken when Pringle, waiting in the queue as 'Lord Chumleigh', experienced a moment of role confusion and mysteriously reverted to being Anna's Dad, ordering her to go back home immediately. . . . The audience were delighted by this bizarre turn of events, despite their recognition that its defiance of logic hardly constituted playing by the rules.

A fourth student asked to replace Anna, in the same scene. Once onstage he appeared to lose confidence and had almost nothing to say, but whether intentional or not this behaviour effectively presented the other actors with a new type of problem to deal with. Williams used the fact that this Anna was struggling to make herself understood as evidence that she could only go in if accompanied by a carer – and by this time the sister had already left. But to everyone's astonishment Lucy interceded yet again, this time appearing next to Anna in the queue to announce that *she* was the carer, and that the ticket purchase could now go ahead: 'And don't forget, *my* ticket is free!', she added. Wheeler interrupted this cheerful anarchy to challenge the credibility of what was arguably a somewhat magical innovation – 'Just who are you supposed to be?' – and was told that she was another sister, 'or brother, or auntie, anyone trying to help her, or just somebody trying to get in on a free ticket . . .'.

There was no opportunity for further evaluation or, to the students' obvious disappointment, further interventions, since we were already over time. They did not want to stop, and I was very aware of those others who were just getting to a point where they could find the courage to enter the performance space. But they were happy to be reminded that they would soon be creating their own Forum play. The members of the film crew were impressed and in some cases evidently taken aback by both the quality of the play and the ability of the spectators to engage with it. Perhaps initially somewhat disconcerted that Heslop – their main object of interest, after all – was so frequently removed from the scene, they became thoroughly absorbed in the improvised dramas that unfolded before them.

Haycliffe School, Bradford (14 July 2003)

Haycliffe is a co-educational secondary school for pupils with learning difficulties, emotional and behavioural difficulties and physical disabilities. Mind the Gap has successfully worked there in the past, and on this occasion were collaborating with SFX to use *Never Again!* as a starting point from which pupils would create their own Forum play later in the year. Haycliffe has been particularly supportive to the arts; the school received a three-year award from the Arts Council of England under their 'Artsmark' scheme to help develop arts provision and demonstrate, as Education Bradford's website puts it, that 'there is more to life than SATs [Scholastic Assessment Tests]' (http://www. educationbradford.com). Artsmark aims to foster community links as well as support activities within a school; this partnership project with Mind the Gap and SFX, examining issues of access to theatre, fits the remit ideally.

Never Again! was performed in Haycliffe's drama studio-cum-sports hall, to an audience of twenty-four pupils aged about sixteen, with two teachers also in attendance. The pupils were evidently excited by the prospect of a play, and a few eagerly reintroduced themselves to Mind the Gap as students who had participated in previous summer schools or other projects. The performance itself was entertaining and energetic, and incorporated a number of slight modifications from its version the previous year: in some cases, particularly effective lines which derived from Forum interventions had been introduced into the actors' standard script. Once the piece had been played through, the Joker – on this occasion, Emma Gee – prepared pupils for the Forum. They were the most immediately forthcoming of any audience I saw, perhaps reflecting the school's enthusiasm and support for arts projects. Gee only needed to ask 'What kinds of things made life difficult for Anna?', to receive a barrage of responses and suggestions as to how to tackle them.

The interventions focused around three areas: home; the box office; the auditorium itself. First up was Ricky, an enthusiastic actor; his first intervention of many was to have Anna climb out of her bedroom window and go on her own – a plan applauded for bravery but problematic since it resulted in Anna being grounded for the foreseeable future. Salim's strategy, which followed, was subtler. He told Mother not to snatch the brochure, which Williams had been doing as part of her character's bossy persona. We waited to see how Salim/Anna would attempt to get her way, but then understood that challenging Mother's manners *was* the intervention. This family had been represented as noisy and competitive; Salim's contribution, slight as it was, shifted the dynamic. This stimulated further ideas. Ricky tried extreme politeness, and Clare asked if she could go with a friend; both got their way.

Salim gave further lessons in manners, once at the box office, to Williams' patronising receptionist: 'What are you shouting for?'. This produced a spontaneous apology, a small but genuine triumph. Meera tried next, combating unhelpfulness with the demand to see the manager. On this occasion the scene was improvised, with Clay in role. When the receptionist's attitude became obviously impertinent he took evident pleasure in firing her, to audience cheers. This decisiveness infected later interventions in the auditorium scene. Ricky, irrepressible as ever, told the complaining spectator loudly to shut up; this led to Anna being asked to leave by the usher. Salim intervened for the third time, with his – now trademark – appeal for tolerance; when the spectator continued to grumble, the usher asked *her* to leave. Finally in this scene, Joe/Anna and the spectator launched into a heated argument, whereupon the usher (Heslop, enjoying new-found power) ejected them both. Gee had to interrupt at this point as time had run out, even though there were at least five hands in the air from pupils desperate to contribute; these last suggestions were shared in discussion. It was evident, from other interventions I've not described, that some pupils did not have a clear idea of a change to make but simply wanted to be in the scene. Once or twice a spect-actor went onstage and essentially replicated an earlier intervention rather than adding something new. This does not seem to me to undermine the Forum. Not everyone was ready to rewrite the play; but most, if not all, could rewrite their relationship to the play.

CONCLUSIONS

Going . . . Going . . . Gone . . . and *Never Again!* are self-evidently very different projects in terms of context, issues examined and target audience. As pieces of Forum Theatre, however, their structures and ambitions are broadly comparable. Both creative processes begin with the realities of oppression as experienced by a specific social group. The oppression is then examined in all its complexity, by exploring immediate personal experience and by undertaking wider research appropriate to the subject. Next the findings are transformed into a theatrical fiction that seeks to demonstrate that oppression to an audience who are themselves directly or indirectly affected by it. Crucially, the audience must recognise the action as both true – although dramatically mediated – and urgent. This achieved, the Joker, actors and audience discuss together what must be changed in order that the oppression be overcome and begin the process of transforming the fiction by introducing alternative possibilities. These theatrical explorations are not the conclusion of the event, since the ultimate aim is the transformation of the oppression *in reality*. Boal states that the Forum method stimulates energy for change and that 'afterwards, catalysed [the oppressed] can immediately apply this new energy to their real lives' (1992: 246). But Cardboard Citizens and Mind the Gap do not assume that this transition will occur unaided. Rather, both companies put in place mechanisms designed to foster and support the energy generated by the Forum and help channel it into permanent reform.

While Image Theatre and especially the Rainbow of Desire techniques encourage participants to engage with their own experience very directly by means of images, dynamisations and transformations, Forum Theatre operates more effectively with a degree of distance: it is a social rather than an individual process. In practice this means that when a participant makes an intervention she is not necessarily rehearsing a strategy that she will specifically take forward into her reality. She may stand up to a tyrannical boss in a Forum, for instance, but have no need to do this in daily life. It is possible to view the intervention as a metaphor, 'the boss' representative of any oppressive figure or social force; from this perspective she is not fighting an individual but testing and developing her powers of resistance in a wider sense. But my experience of watching *Going . . . Going . . . Gone . . .* and *Never Again!* seemed to suggest that the value of Forum was more fundamental than this, that the very fact of making interventions is in some ways more important than their actual content. Both Cardboard Citizens and Mind the Gap practise Forum in contexts where oppression, discrimination and inhibition are starkly evident. That these spectators were prepared to participate at all felt like an achievement. This is in no way to underestimate the capacities of the target audiences; it is rather to acknowledge the power of the forces – mental, physical, social – which mediate against participation. Some of Cardboard Citizens' spectators represented themselves as too cynical, weary, bored, uneducated or simply too cool to participate. By contrast, Mind the Gap's audiences were clearly keen, but either were or pretended to be too shy, anxious, inarticulate or physically awkward to do so. In both cases, these forms of resistance were overcome: not by everyone present, and not to the same degree, but sufficiently for a lively and broadly collective exploration of the plays' issues to be possible.

Both companies' actors and Jokers were prepared to modify the Forum process to meet the needs of their audiences. The terms used to introduce the event could be simplified or problematised; a seemingly passive audience could be teased, flattered or provoked into identifying oppressions and the possibility of combating them; reluctance to participate physically could be tackled by extending the discussion phase, or by bringing the 'characters' directly into the audience's own space. What mattered was that the spectators were actively involved in the process. However, there is a need to strike a balance. The rules of Forum are there for a purpose, and if they are too readily abandoned there is a danger of the task becoming blurred, the goals unclear. The instance of spectators replacing characters other than the protagonist provides a useful example. Adrian Jackson commented to me that, while in general he would resist this for fear of the Forum becoming a 'wish-fulfilment fantasy', exceptions could sometimes be made. The real question is what, if anything, might be learned by such a move. He explains that in his view

> Forum is not, nor ever should be, a doctrinaire process – the mediators of it, Joker and actors, should be sensitive human beings responding to the needs of a particular group. Yes, there are a number of important rules, from which if you diverge you may lose sight of the point of the exercise, and you may indeed lose the whole shape of the event; but equally, the reality is that you respond to whoever is in front of you, you work with whatever tools you have in your repertoire.
>
> (Emailed comments, 6 July 2003)

In the example suggested, it is true that if a spectator plays out a more positive interpretation of a care worker role, for instance, this effectively removes difficulties that the protagonist had previously experienced as a stumbling block. On the other hand, the new scene might well reveal something important to all present – not least, to the care workers in the audience – about the way this individual might hope to be treated in a similar situation. In other words, it is still possible to learn from this.

It has been suggested by some commentators (for example George 1995: 45) that Forum Theatre, particularly as practised in the West, has lost any radical edge it initially possessed and become more about helping individuals adapt to a social system – which is itself left unchallenged – than urging a 'rehearsal of revolution'. The two projects discussed in this chapter show Forum used neither for adaptation nor revolution as such, but towards creative and critical engagement. Cardboard Citizens' own Engagement Programme exemplifies this. Their aim is not to persuade those who have 'dropped out' of society's institutions to fit back into them, but rather to show that disengagement is not their only possibility. They offer a variety of opportunities and alternatives to homeless people, but beyond this issue an invitation: are these useful to you? If not, what would be? What would make a positive difference to your life? In this way, their audiences can be shapers of genuine change. The Forum of *Never Again!* discussed above took place in a different context and had a different purpose, but like *Going . . Going . . . Gone . . .* this project aimed to exert a concrete effect on social systems as well as to develop the capacities of individual audience members to recognise and demand their rights. *Never Again!* was distinctive in that it consciously targeted two audiences: young people, especially those with learning difficulties; and the managers and personnel of arts venues. In line with Mind the Gap's consistent company policy, the In*clu*edo project sought to achieve a bridging between these groups in order to reach a better understanding of a shared problem and ways to address it. To this end, both parties have to accept responsibility: neither one can resolve the issue in isolation.

4

WORKSHOP
PROCESS

Boal uses a vast range of practical exercises, many of which are documented in his books. *Games for Actors and Non-Actors* in particular provides a wealth of these and is extremely accessible. *The Rainbow of Desire* is another important source of approaches, principally intended as a means of exploring personal and psychological issues through theatre. Additionally, Boal is constantly inventing or reinventing others. In any workshop he is likely to introduce a new game and ask participants to judge its usefulness: what does it achieve, and how might it be improved or modified? In this chapter I have included a selection of techniques I have found productive and enjoyable, and have structured these to suggest one way a practical session, or series of sessions, might proceed. I have deliberately introduced a fairly wide range of approaches. It will not necessarily be appropriate to include all these in any one workshop. I have explained how exercises are carried out in my own words, but quote Boal at those moments when illustrations of his distinctive teaching style may prove enlightening. Finally, I have not described or envisaged a specific kind of participant but have tried to show how these techniques can be practised by any interested individual or group, adapting them as the need arises.

FUNDAMENTALS

Of course, those wishing to test out this practice must reflect on the immediate context of their exploration. Consider first the people involved: who, and how many, are the workshop participants? It is probably easiest to work in a fairly small group, but you may not have the luxury of choice – and if you do have large numbers to include, be heartened by the knowledge that Boal regularly runs classes with forty or fifty people and would be unlikely to refuse one double that size in circumstances of necessity. A careful selection of exercises – for example including those that emphasise looking, listening and reflecting as well as doing – will make this more manageable. Second, you need to establish whether there is to be a workshop leader, or leaders. Of course it is an option for a group to proceed through a selection of exercises without leadership, but it is more difficult. As with any training method, it is an advantage to have somebody who is familiar with the approach to oversee the process, make proposals and observe and assist participants' progress.

You should also consider what you already know about the participants. Are you all members of the same community, in broad terms, or from different communities? It is possible to practise the work in both ways, but it is crucial to be aware of the distinction. A relatively homogeneous group will almost certainly be better able to identify issues of shared importance and explore these collectively than a more diverse group, who could learn a great deal from one another but may find it harder to achieve a consensus of priorities. If, on the other hand, your intention is for one defined group to lead the work with another defined group – for instance, for theatre students to run workshops for school children – the leaders should be careful not to pre-judge what the concerns of participants might be. If the leaders perceive themselves to be somehow 'separate' from the participants and their lives, it is unlikely the group as a whole will work effectively together. Finally, it is useful to consider the differences present within any cohort of people, for example of gender, race, age or physical ability. Theatre of the Oppressed techniques are very flexible; they are designed to be inclusive, and there is no set standard that everyone is aiming to achieve. Nevertheless, it is important to establish an atmosphere where participants understand that this is the case and where all work, at whatever level, is valued and respected.

There are further matters to consider, such as the duration and scope of the project. How many sessions are planned and of what length? Do you aim to create a performance of some kind, or are you happy to remain at the level of exploratory process? Ideally you will be as open as possible, allowing the work itself to suggest the form best able to support it. This requires confidence and trust, but is likely to create more satisfactory results than pushing towards a pre-planned outcome when the material the group offers is pulling another way. The importance of trust, accompanied by care and generosity towards one another, can hardly be over-emphasised. Boal's methods offer a way to examine issues of power and oppression as they impact upon your own life; you are asked to engage with your immediate experiences and those of others, to enter territory that may prove difficult or painful. It is impossible to anticipate those experiences or the feelings attached to them. This does not mean that you should be afraid of the work, but simply that your ambitions should be appropriate for the participants, hours and space that you have. It can take time for some people to understand something that is instantly resonant to others, and it is easy to miss the significance of what is in front of you if you believe you already know what you are looking for.

Finally, you should consider what material resources you require. What kind of space is available? It is not necessary to have a theatre studio: how could it be, when at the heart of Theatre of the Oppressed is the desire that no one should be excluded from its practice? Indeed, spaces that are not purpose-built for theatre may prove more interesting, since they often have more character and contain architectural features or objects that can be incorporated into the session. Working in a school classroom, complete with chairs, desks and whiteboard, will be a qualitatively different experience from working with the same children in the studio or sports hall. Some exercises invite participants to make conscious use of the room's characteristics and contents (see, for example, The great game of power (Exercise 4.11, p. 118) and Take your place (Exercise 4.12, p. 119)). However, in the end any space will do, providing it is large enough to hold all those involved. As with any practical session, you should take precautions to ensure that your work will be physically safe. If there is too little room for participants to run, a game of chase is inappropriate. Alternatively, do as Boal does and reinvent the games you want to use to suit the conditions: a slow-motion race, for instance.

WORKSHOP STRUCTURE

In *Theatre of the Oppressed* Boal outlines the following structure for approaching practical work:

Stage 1: *Knowing the body* – simple exercises exploring the body's capabilities and limitations;

Stage 2: *Making the body expressive* – games designed to free the body and imagination;

Stage 3: *The theatre as language* – active engagement with theatrical forms, for example Simultaneous Dramaturgy, Image Theatre and Forum Theatre;

Stage 4: *The theatre as discourse* – additional forms, including Invisible Theatre and Newspaper Theatre, which can be used by spect-actors according to their needs.

(1979: 126)

Games for Actors and Non-Actors maintains the basic principles that inform this structure but suggests a different organisation. Acknowledging that 'there is a fair proportion of exercise in the games and a fair proportion of game in the exercises' (1992: 60), Boal here places greater emphasis on the importance of the senses. He gives five categories of activities:

1 *Feeling what we touch*;
2 *Listening to what we hear*;
3 *Dynamising several senses*;
4 *Seeing what we look at*;
5 *The memory of the senses*.

Within each of these there are sub-categories. *Feeling what we touch*, for example, is broken down further into General exercises, Walks, Massages, Integration games and Gravity; *Listening to what we hear* includes Rhythm, Melody, Sound, Rhythms of respiration and Internal rhythms. *Dynamising several senses* brings aspects of the previous work together, for example in exercises using blindfolds and encouraging sensitivity to sounds, space and each other. Image Theatre techniques are introduced through the fourth category, *Seeing what we look at*. This body of work begins with mirror exercises and moves from there into sculpting, image creation and character games. *The memory of the senses* takes this further still, leading participants to make images expressing specific subjects, including their own experiences. From this point the work can pursue whatever direction feels promising, using any of the more developed forms included within the Theatre of the Oppressed 'arsenal'.

If you have limited time to explore the practice of Theatre of the Oppressed it is more important to take on board general principles than adhere strictly to category divisions – not least because, as Boal points out, all of these necessarily overlap. From my own experience with the work, I suggest including the following basic elements: preparing the body, both individually and in interaction; use of games, to build energy and focus and introduce issues of power; creation of images, and their dynamisation and transformation through sound, movement and action; and exploration of participants' own themes, using the theatrical forms judged most appropriate.

PREPARATION AND GAMES

It is always important for participants to warm up before carrying out extensive practical work in order to minimise the risk of injury. But in Theatre of the Oppressed, this stage also carries ideological significance. How people move and speak, and their degree of freedom or inhibition, may be understood in general as well as individual terms. Our work habits, for example, and the environments we live in, affect our bodies in important ways. We can only begin from where we are – but in order to reach beyond this place, or transform it, we must learn how to extend our physical capabilities as well our minds. In this way even the simplest exercises represent opportunities to become more aware of our selves and how we are affected by personal and social circumstances.

The exercises described are designed to be carried out in silence, unless otherwise stated. If you are leading and are aware that some people are talking at inappropriate moments, try to find out why this might be happening rather than just telling them to be quiet; they may not have understood the exercise, or may be using chatting, or laughter, as a way of expressing nervousness or resistance to the work. If you create opportunities for discussion in between exercises this should help encourage attentiveness during them. Boal always invites reflections on the work as it proceeds; rather than tell participants what an exercise is 'for', he is more likely simply to ask: 'How was it?'.

Exercise 4.1: The cross and the circle

➤ Draw a circle in the air using your right hand. Next, draw a cross, using your left hand. Both of these are simple to do. Now try to do both things at once – and suddenly it is not so easy. Boal frequently uses this as his very first exercise, since it can be performed in groups of any size and generally reduces all participants to a similar position of laughing incompetence. Why should the exercise be so difficult when there is no physiological barrier? What psychological factors are at work?

Exercise 4.2: Minimum surface contact

➤ Working on your own, explore the ways in which you can have minimum surface contact with the floor. Can you stand just on the toes or the heel of one foot? Can you balance on one knee and one finger? Keep moving, trying to discover the full range of possibilities available to you, making sure that every part of your body becomes involved. Notice the unfamiliarity of some of these positions, the weight of your torso and limbs, how gravity pulls you to the floor and how far you are able to resist.

Exercise 4.3: Columbian hypnosis

➤ This is a very good exercise through which to introduce ideas of power and responsibility, simultaneously providing a gentle yet thorough physical warm up. It is a pair exercise, but is easy to modify if you have odd numbers. A and B stand facing one another. A raises one hand and positions it, palm forward, a few centimetres away from her partner's face (as if her hand were a mirror the other is looking into). B remains 'hypnotised' by A's hand, his task to maintain this same distance – so if A moves her hand in any direction, B must adjust his position accordingly. A can move wherever she wants: she can reach up high or place her hand on the floor, walk around the room, change pace. Her aim is to encourage her partner to stretch, turn and bend – to become increasingly responsive to even the tiniest changes. A must take good care of her partner; she should not force B into positions which are clearly uncomfortable, or move so suddenly that he has no hope of keeping up. To this end it is advisable to begin the exercise very slowly. This helps establish concentration, and makes it easier to keep a safe distance from other couples in the room. After a few minutes, A and B swap roles and the exercise is repeated; once again, start slowly.

Variation 1

➤ The same exercise, but with A's hand movements reduced to the minimum. Take the exercise down to its subtlest level: how sensitive can both the leader's impulses and follower's responses be?

Variation 2

➤ The same exercise, but in groups of three. A guides B and C simultaneously, using both hands. The followers may be led to move as if they were mirrors of each other, may cross over each other, may be held apart; the leader decides. Swap over twice, to give each person a chance to guide the others.

Variation 3

➤ The same exercise, in larger groups or as a whole group. Different parts of the leader's body are used as hypnotic focus as well as the hand, such as the back, shoulder, knee or chest. Try varying the distance the followers stand from A. In this version, the followers find that they must work even harder: for A to turn 90° may be a small movement, but someone standing six or more feet away will have to travel much further to maintain the same physical relationship.

Exercise 4.4: Pushing against each other

➤ Work in pairs, facing one another, hands on your partner's shoulders. Imagine there is a line between you on the floor. Each of you must push as hard as you can, but neither is allowed to cross the line. If one of you feels that you are 'winning', you should reduce the pressure. The aim is not so much to balance against each other as continually to negotiate the force exerted between you. Boal comments that the exercise mirrors what the player in Forum must do, 'neither give way to the intervening spect-actor, nor overwhelm him, but rather help him to apply all his strength' (1992: 66).

Variation 1

➤ The same principle but with other parts of the body, for example back to back, bottom to bottom, shoulder to shoulder.

Variation 2

➤ The same principle, but with added movement. Begin the exercise back to back, but this time 'walk' down until you are both sitting on the floor, maintaining back contact all the time. Stand up again, still keeping contact. You should not need to touch the floor with your hands at any point.

Variation 3

➤ Sit on the floor facing your partner, legs straight out in front, feet to feet. Reach forward and hold each other's arms. Stand up together, using your respective weights to find the balance that makes this possible.

Variation 4

➤ The same exercise as 3, but in this variation A uses her weight to pull B to her feet, then B sinks back down, pulls and A rises. This creates a 'seesaw' effect – and, as on a real seesaw, there will be a mid-point when both A and B will be halfway up.

Exercise 4.5: Slow-motion race

➤ This exercise is just what it says. Participants 'run' as slowly as possible, the winner being the last person to cross the finishing line. But there are rules: you must keep moving forwards, and you can only have one foot on the floor at a time, and the raised foot must pass above knee height. Like the preceding exercises, this one requires a combination of strength and balance and is surprisingly hard work.

Exercise 4.6: The bomb and the shield

➤ This simple exercise creates a high level of energy and excitement.
Walk around the room, as a group. Each participant chooses two
other people, in her mind: one as a 'bomb', the other as a 'shield'.
At a signal from the workshop leader, each moves to try to place
her shield between herself and her bomb. This causes instant
chaos, since everyone has different priorities; your bomb may
even have chosen you to be his shield. Often the group finds a
temporarily 'settled' position, only for a slight adjustment from
one person to set it all off again. You can conclude this exercise
with a countdown from 10 to 1, a last chance for everyone to shield
herself safely.

Exercise 4.7: Fainting by numbers

➤ Members of the group are given a number each, from 1 to 10.
If there are more than ten people, begin again so that there are two
1s, two 2s and so on. Walk around the room keeping fairly close
together, observing each other carefully. The workshop leader calls
out a number – say 4 – and those with that number 'faint', but must
be safely caught by the other participants before they reach the
floor. Of course, this exercise needs to be handled carefully to avoid
accidents and one useful rule is that those fainting must pause
before they fall; you can incorporate a deliberately exaggerated
in-breath or raised arm as a signal, or a subtler moment of unsteadi-
ness, or gesture of the hand to the head. This exercise is a very
good way to build focus. It is hard to remember who has which
number, so in reality when any number is called everybody else is
put instantly on alert, scanning faces and bodies for any hints of
imminent collapse.

Exercise 4.8: The bear of Poitiers

➤ This is one of the many children's games that Boal incorporates
into practical training. Others you may know include grandmother's
footsteps, stick-in-the-mud, and cat and mouse. Some of these
games are based on speed and quick reflexes, others on stealth. I
find The bear of Poitiers a particularly useful one to include, since
it combines simple rules with plenty of room for improvisation.

➤ One person is the bear, the others woodcutters. The bear turns his back on the woodcutters, who are at work in the forest chopping trees, talking, singing. Then the bear lets out a roar: the instant this happens the woodcutters fall to the ground and lie there motionless, since it is known that bears will not attack dead bodies. The bear wanders through the forest and inspects the bodies, touching them, tickling, roaring, breathing on them, trying every trick (short of talking) to discover whether they are really dead. If a woodcutter reveals herself to be alive – for example by moving, or laughing – she becomes a bear too and joins the search for victims. The winner of the game is the last woodcutter to be caught by the bears. However, you may have to end the game before this, since it frequently happens that those people who do not immediately give way under the bear's inspection are able to lie still almost indefinitely, their minds uncannily detached from the action.

Exercise 4.9: Carnival in Rio

➤ This is a vibrant, energetic exercise that involves everybody and encourages participants to fill all available space with movement and sound. It is a good idea to precede this exercise with some other, simpler ones involving rhythm. Boal gives a great many to choose from which use clapping, gestures, noises, song and so on (1992: 88–101).

➤ Form groups of three and stand side by side in a line. On instruction by the workshop leader, person A begins a lively rhythmic sound and physical action, which she then repeats. B and C copy this as exactly as they can, so that all three are producing the same rhythm. Next, B is invited to create his own sound and action, which A and C learn and imitate. Finally, it is C's turn to do the same. Now each group of three knows three different rhythms. The workshop leader gives the instruction 'Return to your original rhythms!', whereupon each participant picks up her own created rhythm and the room is filled with the greatest possible variety of sound and movement. Then the instruction comes to 'Unify!' and each group of three must choose which of its rhythms to settle on collectively. This must be negotiated *while you are doing it*, without any discussion. Once unified, the groups move around the room, each producing its own rhythm. After a while, the workshop leader gives the instruction 'You may change groups!' to allow anyone who prefers another group's rhythm to adopt that one instead. Eventually, there is a final instruction for the group as a whole to 'Unify!', and all participants join together to create a single rhythm.

IMAGES AND EXPERIENCE

Exercise 4.10: Complete the image

➤ This exercise is an excellent lead-in to Image Theatre work, as it encourages physical expressiveness and spontaneity without the pressure of a specific theme to focus upon. Work in pairs. A and B stand and face each other. Shake hands – and freeze in that position. A then steps out of the pose, while B remains frozen, arm outstretched. A takes up a new position in relation to B, thereby creating a new total image. Now A freezes and B steps out. B then takes up another position, in relation to that of A. A and B continue to take turns in this way, together improvising a series of possible relationships. The images that are created may be broadly representational, or expressions of abstract physicality. For example A might respond to B standing with outstretched hand (the first image) by dropping to her knees in front of B as if she is being blessed; alternatively she might choose to copy the pose, but standing alongside her partner. It can be liberating to be allowed to work in non-representational ways. Certain images may suggest a context to you – for example, a raised arm might imply a blow about to be struck – but others are likely to leave you blank; in these contexts it is better to move swiftly into a pose which is physically appealing but which you think 'means' nothing than to hesitate and struggle for an idea. It takes time to understand how this exercise works in practice, so after an initial short trial and response, you may want to let it run for several minutes.

Observation and reflection

➤ This is a particularly rewarding exercise to watch. After you have all practised it, try having half the pairs work while the others observe. Those working should be performing the exercise anew, not trying to recreate the same set of images they produced the first time around. Those watching can study the relationships suggested by each pair – the movement 'dialogues' which emerge. Often pairs seem to pursue a single relationship dynamic across a whole series of images, a repeated pattern of application and rejection, for example; there seems to be an implied narrative underlying their actions. Some pairs tend towards the comic, others to symbolic violence; others find a language close to dance. Notice especially the subtle – and not so subtle – shifts of power which take place: one person may tower threateningly over another, but if the latter simply moves away they leave their former 'oppressor' frozen in a pose which appears motiveless and suddenly vulnerable. This principle of fluidity and dynamism is fundamental to the Theatre of the Oppressed. Images are not static but always open to interrogation, just like the realities they represent.

Exercise 4.11: The great game of power

➤ This exercise invites participants to examine issues of power and representation in a more direct way than previously, but without the necessity of confronting these on an immediate and personal level. Boal's version uses a table, six chairs and a plastic bottle, but you could modify this depending on what you have available in the space (see photographs of the game in action in Boal 1992: 151–5). The workshop leader invites participants to come up in turn and arrange the objects in such a way as to make one chair seem more powerful than all the others. The group examine and discuss each arrangement as it is made. The leader asks for further arrangements, which will make that chair even more powerful than in previous versions. Eventually the group are asked to settle for one particularly powerful configuration. Once this is set up, anyone who chooses can enter the space and assume what he considers to be the most powerful position possible. Then a second person enters and attempts to take away the power of the first by establishing a more powerful position. The game continues with a third and a fourth until as many participants as possible are in the space.

Observation and reflection

➤ Try to create maximum opportunity for participation in this exercise. When the initial arrangements are invited, everyone can take a turn at creating their representation of power; if anyone seems not to have an idea, she can be encouraged to repeat – and thus reinforce – an earlier proposal. The purpose of the exercise is to explore ways in which power is manifested, how it can become oppression, how it can be overthrown. The series of images created by the group will express these ideas in symbolic terms. Different forms of power emerge: rule by force versus rule by consensus, for example. When the space begins to be populated by human beings as well as objects, some of the transformative possibilities of Complete the image (Exercise 4.10, p. 117) reappear. The teacher sitting at her desk loses authority when a pupil stands and threatens her with a chair; a third person who starts laughing at the pupil may seem more in control than either. As with many Theatre of the Oppressed techniques, participants are encouraged to show their ideas physically first of all, then seek responses from the others.

Exercise 4.12: Take your place

➤ I find this exercise most interesting with a group who already know each other, or think that they do, but you can use it in any context. It runs as follows. The workshop leader instructs participants to choose 'your ideal place' within the room – the place where you would most like to be, where you feel happiest – and to occupy that place. The next instruction is to do the opposite, to identify 'your most hated place' and go to that one in its turn. The final instruction is to take up 'your true place'. After each stage, the workshop leader can invite participants to reflect on the choices they made and share their thoughts with the group.

➤ Simple as it is, this exercise can prove extremely powerful. Although participants are determining individually where they will move, their decisions affect and are affected by the rest of the group. In the first stage you might select a quiet corner as your ideal place, but on finding that three others converge upon it simultaneously it may lose its appeal; alternatively, you may discover that sharing the place makes it more pleasurable than if you had it just for yourself. Looking around, you may be surprised where some players choose to go. Often the most frequent contributors 'ideally' take up a place on the periphery, while those who can seem more passive are nevertheless happiest in the centre of events. If you have time, it is worth giving each person the opportunity to explain his choice; there is something about the ritualistic qualities of the exercise that seems to encourage openness and honesty. The change of atmosphere between the first and second stages is palpable. The room seems to grow colder as participants disperse, turn their backs, or – in some cases – force themselves grimly into the most exposed area of the space. Once again, the choices made can be surprising. Participants are often puzzled by the third instruction, unsure what is meant by their 'true' place. But there can be no further explanation, only a different way of asking people to make the same decision: 'There is a place in the room which is yours – where is it?'. Participants may interpret the challenge in different ways, but each must come up with an answer. Some people return to their ideal place, as if they believe it is rightfully theirs. Others take up new places altogether, expressive of how they see themselves at that moment. A few people usually move into the centre of the space to form a kind of neutral, waiting group – as if to suggest, perhaps, that their true place is something they will necessarily have to negotiate with others.

Variation

➤ Exactly as before, except that Take your place is preceded by the creation of images around the room using furniture, objects and characteristics of the space itself. This could follow on from The great game of power (Exercise 4.11, p. 118), so that participants have already had some experience of making arrangements that are expressive of hierarchies, authority, control or rebellion. The more cluttered the space is originally, the better; people can take turns to use anything that's there – chairs, coats, a ladder, bunches of keys – to create what are literally 'power structures'. This exercise is valuable in itself, as it encourages imagination and confidence in playing with available materials and develops skills in symbolic expression, but as a preface to Take your place it serves the additional function of creating a playing environment that is already loaded with meanings. Having said this, the most neutral-seeming space can be 'read' for its significance. This variation simply presents a different route into the work and of course stimulates a different set of results.

Exercise 4.13: The image of the word

➤ You might use this exercise in the early stages of Image Theatre work, since it introduces some of its simplest principles. It is also a useful technique to draw on as a means of assessing the resonance certain themes might hold for a particular group of people.

Image creation

➤ Participants stand in a circle, facing outwards. The workshop leader announces a word or phrase, for example 'riches', 'happiness', 'the boss', 'Christmas', 'theatre' – whatever might seem to be relevant or provocative. This is the subject to be illustrated. Each participant considers in her own mind how she will express this theme in a still image, using her own body. This decided, she turns around. Turning back to face the group serves as a signal to the workshop leader; once everyone is looking inwards, we are ready to begin. On the count of three, all participants form their images simultaneously. Even from this frozen position, it is usually possible for people to observe each other: how has the concept of 'riches', for instance, been diversely interpreted?

➤ The workshop leader instructs participants to move towards others whose images resemble their own. Some images may remain distinctive and separate, but generally families of images also begin to form. The aim is not to find images which are identical, but which use common shapes or appear to carry a similar feeling. At this stage, participants are making these judgements on the basis of physicality alone. Once this has been done, it is possible to examine each sub-group in turn and for interpretations to be offered by those observing. These people should look carefully, taking account of every detail: tensions, gestures, expressions. By this process of examination and commentary, participants train one another to be more noticing 'readers' and more precise creators of images. Those within the images do not interrupt to support or correct the observers' impressions, but simply listen.

Dynamisation

➤ Once all the images have been discussed, they can be dynamised. This can be done one image at a time, or a sub-group at a time; the latter is likely to be less intimidating for a new group. Dynamisation occurs on three levels: movement, sound and action. Each stage is an opportunity to discover more about the idea being expressed.

➤ The workshop leader asks each person or sub-group: 'If your image could make a movement, what would that be?'. On the count of three, the images come briefly to life. One stamps its foot; another makes a pleading gesture; a third turns its back on the others; and so on. The movement can be repeated several times, to give it time to register with the observers. Do these movements confirm or challenge earlier interpretations?

➤ The second invitation is made: 'What would your image say if it could speak?' or 'What sound would your image make if it had a voice?'. This oral phase of dynamisation can be introduced in different ways. Participants can be asked to offer a sound, a single word or phrase, or a stream of consciousness monologue – again, on the count of three. All of these can work powerfully. It's important for participants to understand that they need not be a character, speaking to an imaginary other character; the aim of the exercise is rather to grant power of speech to the image. As before, the words or sounds chosen may alter the observers' original perceptions. By this time, it may even be apparent that one or more images do not really belong to that sub-group; there may be a physical resemblance, but the spirit is quite contrary to the majority.

➤ The third invitation proposes action: 'What does your image do next?'. In other words, if it were not rooted to the spot what would its actions be? This phase is the most complex, since it can involve interaction as well as action. While the dynamisation of certain images will be effectively solitary, some will impinge on others: aggressive images may seek out confrontation, unhappy ones may look for comfort, and so on. Once again, the observers must pay close attention, never assuming that they already know what an image is trying express.

➤ When each stage has been carried out once it can be useful to reconstruct what took place. The first round is likely to be slow, especially if participants are new to the exercise. Second time through the workshop leader can put the elements together, asking for 'Images! Movements! Sound! Action!' in swift succession. This speeded up version, of course, moves the exercise closer to the continuous energy of theatrical performance.

➤ Once the components of the exercise have been understood, it is possible to play with their arrangement in various ways. The workshop leader may think it better for the group to make images of several words, for example, before dynamising one. And once dynamisation has been practised once, it is helpful to do it again, with new words; like any technique, it takes time to learn how to use it effectively. Participants should be given the chance to suggest words or themes of their own, as this helps establish which ideas might carry potency for which groups. The same principles are used in another, more developed form of dynamisation: The three wishes (Exercise 4.15, p. 125).

Exercise 4.14: Sculpting

➤ As well as asking participants to make their own images Boal frequently uses sculpting, whereby ideas are expressed using the bodies of others. Sculpting is a valuable technique for several reasons. It requires sensitive physical interaction, prepared for by earlier exercises such as Pushing against each other (Exercise 4.4, p. 113) and Columbian hypnosis (Exercise 4.3, p. 112). It develops physical communication skills, since 'sculptors' must use these rather than words to give shape to their 'clay'. It helps participants sharpen their own powers of image-making, since they learn from a position of observation how effectively their ideas are being expressed. It can also engender a useful resistance on the part of the people being sculpted, for while they may submit their bodies to the sculpting process their minds may rebel against the pose they are required to adopt. If this is articulated, it will reveal the tensions, reflections and emotions stirred in the participants by the material. Alternatively, this energy can be channelled through the production of counter-images. Further, the recognition that someone might want actively to *resist* the image in which they have been placed goes to the very heart of Theatre of the Oppressed: it is a small step from here to the protagonist of Forum Theatre, for example.

➤ The sculpting techniques themselves can take a variety of forms, some of which are indicated below.

The sculptor touches the model

➤ Participants form pairs, A and B. A sculpts B into her chosen interpretation of the agreed theme, trying to be as precise as possible in the physical signals she gives to B. B is not a dead weight, but malleable; the exercise is not about forcing your partner into a position, but about sensitive communication and reception. Once all the images have been created, they can be studied as a group. As usual, the emphasis is placed on the observers' perceptions; this is almost always likely to be more revealing than if the sculptor herself explains what it's 'meant to be'. The partners swap over, and it is B's turn to sculpt A – expressing the same theme, or a new theme.

The sculptor doesn't touch the model

➤ This version follows the same pattern as previously but, rather than using hands-on touching, A stands a short distance away from B. This time A 'sculpts' by gesture alone: she does not adopt a pose for B to copy but uses her own body to send impulses to B, to which he responds as truthfully as he is able. A's gestures remain realistic; she does the same movements she used in the previous version, if somewhat heightened in order to communicate across the physical gap.

The sculptors shape a group image

➤ Here, one sculptor creates an image using her partner on the chosen theme. A second sculptor adds to it, then a third, and so on until a collective image has been produced.

A single sculptor shapes a group image

➤ As the title suggests, individual sculptors take turns to create simple or complex images expressing their own interpretations of the chosen theme. These may be based on personal experience (see The image of oppression, Exercise 4.16, p. 126) or simply on observation and imagination. As always, different ways of introducing the exercise will encourage different responses.

➤ Any images created by these processes can be dynamised using the stages described in The image of the word (Exercise 4.13, p. 121). But of course the difference here is that the people who inhabit the images may not know what their creators intended them to express. They only know what they feel. So their movements, speech and action may bring the image to life, or it may reveal their *attitude* to their image; both kinds of response will be informative.

Exercise 4.15: The three wishes

➤ This technique can be applied to an image or set of images. It can also be used as a modified version of Forum Theatre. It is similar to the action stage of The image of the word (Exercise 4.13, p. 121), but offers a more structured way to examine what might 'happen next'. Beyond this, it asks not simply what *does* happen, but what we *want* to happen: hence the wishes.

➤ Take as an example the theme 'the couple'. The participants have created a series of interpretations of this idea: there is a loving couple, a warring couple, an image which contains three people, another which has just one. The workshop leader can stimulate diversity by letting participants sculpt images in turn, after each asking: 'This is one couple – who can show us a *different* couple?'.

➤ As explained in relation to the Sculpting series (Exercise 4.14, pp. 123–4), those inside the images may not necessarily feel 'at home' there. Within the 'couple' images they may be placed in positions of aggression or unhappiness, or they may experience a 'happy' image as sentimental or claustrophobic. These attitudes are revealed through the process of dynamisation. The workshop leader explains that each person has three wishes, each 'wish' taking the form of a gesture or action: so if someone wants to transform or abandon her 'couple' she has three opportunities to physicalise this. The dynamisations happen on the count of three. However, all participants make their wishes simultaneously. This means that one person's wish may well conflict with another's. If this occurs participants have to make choices, as in life: they can pursue their original wish, find their own to be changed by the wishes of others, or subordinate their own desires altogether. The exercise bears some resemblance to Take your place (Exercise 4.12, p. 119): individual choices can be affected in surprising ways by the actions of others. With all these dynamisation exercises, it is often helpful to reconstruct the process for further examination. Here it is usually possible to identify sub-groups of individuals who interacted with one another; who can recreate the stages they passed through while the others observe.

➤ This dynamisation by means of 'wishes' highlights another important principle of Theatre of the Oppressed. The animations that occur in this exercise do not simply bring an image to life, but are about changing that image to express a new reality in which participants feel happier or more empowered. Boal talks of the *real*, the *ideal* and the *transitional*. We make an image of reality, a reality that may be oppressive. We have an image in our minds of that reality ideally transformed. But in order to move from the *real* towards the *ideal* we must go through a *transition*, or series of transitions. The embodiment of this idea is what makes Theatre of the Oppressed a 'rehearsal of revolution', in Boal's terms, rather than a staging of utopias; if we cannot identify the steps that could be taken to make the ideal our new reality it remains a fantasy rather than a stimulus to change.

Exercise 4.16: The image of oppression

Preparation

➤   This extended exercise offers one route into working with partici- pants' own experiences of oppression. The process needs to be introduced with care. Often people find the very word 'oppression' off-putting, for a variety of reasons. While some might simply be reluctant to engage with serious issues, others will feel that they have never encountered oppression, or that it is a word that should be reserved to describe societies where abuse of power is consis- tently manifest and violent. One way to circumvent this is to change the terms of the question. Rather than ask: 'Can you remember an occasion when you felt oppressed?', you might ask: 'Have you ever been in a situation where you felt powerless?'. Alternatively, partici- pants could spend some time exploring what 'oppression' means. This can be done practically (for example through The great game of power, Exercise 4.11, p. 118) and by means of discussion. Once it is acknowledged that the term carries connotations of 'restric- tion', as well as tyranny and physical force, it becomes easier for participants to see ways in which oppression is present in their own lives. Ideas are freed up still further if people understand that they may be their *own* 'oppressors' – they are not obliged to see themselves as the victims of others.

➤   The exercise proceeds as follows. Participants find a place on their own in the room, and close their eyes. The workshop leader asks each person to recall a situation when they felt powerless; this could have happened earlier that day, last week, ten years earlier – the date is unimportant. What *is* important is that the experience mattered; that it is still possible to remember the feelings it conjured. (The workshop leader can give assurances that no one will be obliged to share the details of these if they prefer not to.) Participants are given a few minutes to bring this experience to mind as vividly as possible.

The images

➤ The group is then divided into sub-groups of four or five. Within each sub-group, participants take turns to 'sculpt' an image of their experience using the bodies of the other three or four people; in every case, the sculptor completes the image by entering it herself, *representing herself*. The images can be literal or symbolic expressions of the experience. The aim is for the sculptor to reveal to the others as vividly as possible – without words – what that experience was like. Once each person has created an image, the groups may wish to 'rehearse' these briefly so that they can move confidently through the whole series without stopping for discussion.

➤ Each sub-group shows the images to the group as a whole. They should be offered slowly, each one held for several seconds to allow time for it to be absorbed. Observers can be invited to 'read' the images as they are presented, but it may prove more effective to maintain silence at this stage and encourage responses on a second showing (if time permits). Those watching are asked to look closely at the image, if appropriate to walk around it and see it from all sides. Discussion should focus on what is there; suggestions might be offered about what the image represents, but it is important that this is not reduced into a simple 'guessing game'.

➤ When all the images have been seen and commented on, the group are asked to identify those that seemed to resonate most strongly. It is likely that several will be suggested. At this point the 'owners' of the images selected can be asked if they are willing to share the experiences which gave rise to them. Let us suppose that three people agree to do this. Participants divide into three groups; each of these will hear one experience recounted. (You can of course vary this procedure, depending on the size of the group and time available.) Imagine that these are the stories shared. A describes a stressful and potentially dangerous work situation where everyone claimed her attention at once. B recalls being forbidden to stay out late as a teenager, while her brother was allowed far more leeway. C remembers the shock he felt when his wife confessed that she had been having an affair and was leaving him. Make sure each group has enough time to hear and respond to the experience being shared. The listeners' role is principally just that – to listen – rather than to offer opinions; they need to understand the story, and its significance for the speaker, as precisely as possible.

The scenes

➤   Next, each group creates a short scene demonstrating the oppression they have discussed. This can be based on the participant's original sculpted image, adding only the movement and words/ sound necessary to clarify its meaning for the spect-actors, or it can be represented in an entirely different way. (An advantage of working from the original image, however, is that it helps to avoid lengthy discussions about the best method of demonstrating the oppression.) As before, the individual who offered the experience may wish to play herself, but this is not a requirement; it is important simply to be aware that the choices made necessarily affect the nature of the material produced, and the relationship of the participants to that material.

➤   Imagine that these three scenes are created and shown. Scene A shows a care assistant working in an old peoples' home. An elderly and disabled resident insists that she help him to the bathroom even though she has already taken him there twice in the last half hour. But before she can do anything, she is interrupted by the relative of another resident who is worried by her mother's complaints of staff inattentiveness. The assistant is caught up in the conversation with the relative; meanwhile the man tries to walk to the bathroom on his own, but falls over on the way and is hurt. Scene B involves a mother and daughter, sitting in a living room. The daughter is ready to go out for the evening, but her mother insists she must be home by eleven. The daughter protests, but mother is adamant; eventually the girl storms up to her bedroom, shouting that if she must be back so soon there is no point in her going out at all. Scene C takes place at a party, with several people present. A man is pulled into a corner by his wife, who has something to tell him that 'can't wait'. In a rush of words, she reveals she has been having an affair. It's no one he knows, she says, and she doesn't even know whether she loves the other man, but she has decided to leave. She starts to cry, saying how sorry she is, that she knows how he must be feeling, and how much she hates hurting him. Her husband stands there, stunned into silence.

Working on the scenes

➤ It is important to recognise that, since The image of oppression technique as described includes few restrictions, it is likely that the *kinds* of experiences participants bring to the workshop will vary considerably. Some versions of oppression may appear to be more 'social' – for example, the story of pressures in the care home; with others seemingly more 'personal' – the other two stories. This is an oversimplification, inevitably, since all three reveal tensions that could be examined in both personal and social terms, but it indicates a difference of emphasis. You could choose to structure the preceding work to lead more decisively towards either one sphere or another, but for the purpose of illustrating the breadth of possibilities Theatre of the Oppressed offers, I have kept this open. What follows here is an outline of three techniques that could be adopted at this point as a way of working on each scene. Of course you will decide what is most appropriate and how much is manageable within the context and ambitions of your own workshop.

Scene A: The care assistant

Technique – Forum Theatre

➤ The scene can be offered to the spect-actors as a simple Forum, following the model described in Chapter 3. How could the care assistant, as protagonist, handle the situation better and prevent the accident occurring? Encourage as many suggestions – preferably in the form of theatrical interventions – as possible. Each is evaluated in turn. Boal usually asks simply: 'Was that progress?'. If so, why? If not, why not? The discussion need not be prolonged *as* discussion, but can be a means to provoke further ideas to try out. If the work proceeds sensitively, the group will move towards a deeper understanding of the scene. For example, while both the first resident and the relative might appear demanding, querulous, even 'oppressive', there are clearly legitimate feelings which prompt their behaviour. Is it possible for the assistant to treat both parties with respect and care, when neither seems very ready to be reasoned with? Each time a spect-actor replaces the protagonist, the other actors improvise their responses to the new intervention. Boal insists that they should not give in easily but rather intensify the oppression, since the Forum game is based upon 'spect-actors – trying to find a new solution, trying to change the world – against actors – trying to hold them back, to force them to accept the world as it is' (1992: 20). Nevertheless, the spect-actors as a body should judge whether the actors are playing fair; it is too dispiriting to fight a hopeless battle! If the other actors genuinely feel the situation has been transformed by an intervention, they must allow themselves to give in.

➤   Like all Theatre of the Oppressed techniques, work with Forum improves with practice. But this is a good place to start: a short scene that is straightforward without being obviously reductive, and an identifiable protagonist whose seeming powerlessness has serious consequences.

Scene B: The teenage daughter

Technique – Boxing seconds

➤   This technique works very effectively with a scene which has as its essence two people engaging in a battle of wills. It seems initially as if the protagonist of this drama must be the daughter, since this was the role of the participant who offered the experience. But it is easily possible to sympathise with both parties in this scenario, and this suggests an opportunity for an approach less geared towards 'helping the protagonist achieve their aim' than towards an outcome whereby both might emerge as 'winners'.

➤   The scene performed once, the spect-actors are asked how far they identify with the two characters they have seen. In this example we could imagine that they have sympathy for them both. Some tend to side with the daughter; they feel that the mother is untrusting and repressive, and guilty of operating a double standard since the girl's brother is permitted far more freedom. Others feel stronger identification with the mother's position; she is afraid for her daughter's safety, and gets no pleasure from imposing what she sees as necessary restrictions. As in Forum Theatre, spect-actors are challenged to explore what it is these *two* protagonists want, and what each might do differently in order to achieve their aim. But in this technique, rather than have them replace the characters, they join them at the edges of the performance space as if they were their seconds in a boxing match. A minimum of two spect-actors must play, one to support each protagonist, but it is possible to bring in as many as want to take part. The timing is important. Having observed the scene the first time around, the seconds have exactly one minute privately to 'coach' their own protagonist; they suggest different ways each could approach the other which might prove more successful. The scene begins again: now the dialogue and action have changed, although as before the daughter's aim is to stay out as late as possible, the mother's to ensure that she is safely home by eleven. After two minutes of the new scene, the workshop leader calls for an end to 'round one'. The seconds rush to the protagonists, having observed their progress. Now they have modifications, or wholly new strategies, to propose. Once again, after a minute, the action starts; and after two minutes, the end of 'round two' is called. The game proceeds in this manner, shifting from coaching to improvisation, more coaching to more improvisation, all towards the goal of achieving an outcome that both protagonists will accept. If the seconds run out of ideas they can drop back into the audience and allow new ones to take over, and if any spect-actors watching the scene feel inspired to join a group of seconds, they are free to do so.

➤ Boxing seconds is an enjoyable exercise to play. Some spect-actors may find it a less intimidating technique than Forum, since they can join in without being required to replace the protagonist or indeed to 'act' in the usual sense of the word. Moreover, participants can intervene with a friend, or as a group; they need not feel individually exposed. Boxing seconds also differs from Forum in that it is more obviously developmental. Rather than existing as a series of contrasting interventions, the changes proposed tend to move the action progressively closer towards the desired end. We can imagine how this works in practice in relation to the scene described above. Perhaps the daughter's seconds advise her first of all to *ask* if she can stay out late, rather than simply try to leave the house and be stopped by her mother. The actress tries this strategy; it fails, since the mother still refuses, but the response she receives is at least more sympathetic. The protagonists return to their seconds for more suggestions. The daughter's supporters urge her to remind her mother of the freedoms allowed her brother and make her see that this inequity is unreasonable. Meanwhile, those backing the mother recommend she tell the girl that it is because she loves her that she is insisting on these rules. The two confront each other again with these new ideas. The actress playing the mother speaks first, and her expressions of love and care rather take the wind out of the other's sails. The latter brings up the different treatment of her brother, as instructed, but even as she does so she recognises that the mother has a point: unfair or not, the risks each face *are* different. The seconds try again. Those with the mother tell the actress that she's doing fine; they feel she has control of the scene. However, the daughter's seconds have decided on a complete change of tactic. In order to get what she wants she will have to calm her mother's anxieties, rather than deny them. They have several ideas: she can offer to stay the night with a friend of whom her mother approves; she can promise that they will take a taxi back home after the party; she can suggest that her mother rings the friend's parents now, to set up the arrangement. After perhaps one or two more rounds, this approach succeeds. The seconds introduce modifications on both sides when they see how the other reacts. As with Forum, neither is too quick to give in but each will allow herself to be persuaded if she judges that an acceptable solution has been reached.

Scene C: The husband

Technique – The kaleidoscopic image

➤ The husband and wife scene is possibly the most emotionally complex of the three described – at least, it seems the most immediately traumatic. It is clearly 'dramatic' but nevertheless difficult to tackle, for a number of reasons. It would be hard to imagine working on the scene through Forum. The husband has been represented as the protagonist, and certainly he feels oppressed in this encounter, but what does he want from it? What possible 'solution' could there be? Forum also feels unsuitable because of the highly personal nature of the experience. If you were he, what would it be like to have others replace you in the belief that they could somehow handle the situation better? The Boxing seconds technique would also be hard to apply, not least because it requires that the spect-actors know what it is both parties are striving for – and the husband here is mute. Above all, it feels important to find out more about the husband's response: his thoughts, impulses and desires. The challenge is not general – what do people want when their partners tell them they are leaving? – but specific: what does *this* man want? Does he even know? In such a situation it is better to consider drawing from the Rainbow of Desire techniques, since they are designed to help explore those internalised oppressions, anxieties and longings that may influence us without our realising it.

➤ The kaleidoscopic image as I describe it is based on Boal's technique of the same name (1995: 96–109). The assumption is made here that the person who first shared the experience plays himself within the action. It runs as follows. First, the actors present the scene as prepared. It will be remembered that this took place at a party, with other people present as well as the husband and wife. But since these others seem in a sense incidental to the action – they are not directly involved in any way – the decision can be taken to remove them, at least temporarily, thus involving just the two principal characters. In the scene as it is, the wife has virtually all the words; it is as if she speaks for both of them. This technique aims to reveal *his* feelings and let these find a voice.

– The images of desires

➤ Once the action has been presented for the first time, the protagonist is invited to construct an image that expresses a 'desire' he feels within that encounter – or one that he felt at the time. He can ask any one of the spect-actors to be the body that he sculpts. For example, he might have felt the desire to cover his ears and block out what his wife was saying; so he sculpts an image that is doing exactly this, and places it within the performance space. He is invited to shape another of his desires. He acknowledges that he is angry with her, almost to the point of violence. This image has his wife by the throat with one hand, the other raised as if to hit. He has a third impulse that is, perhaps bizarrely, to laugh; he cannot believe this is happening, that she can actually be serious. The image of this desire has a grimace that could be one of hilarity or pain, and is holding onto its sides.

➤ If at this point the protagonist does not have any more desires/ images to propose, the invitation to offer further ones can be extended to the spect-actors. This need not be intrusive; it is not a matter of them telling him something he cannot see for himself, but rather of sharing what they themselves felt as they watched the scene – their imaginative engagement with it. Any spect-actor who wishes can shape a desire, offering it to the protagonist as a proposal. Perhaps someone feels that the protagonist longs to clasp his wife in his arms, to claim her as his own and no one else's. Another spect-actor sees disillusionment and bitterness. A third feels like crying. A fourth wants to run away. A fifth has a glimmer of hope, believing that if he can persuade his wife not to leave immediately she might come to change her mind. All of these desires are sculpted into images by the spect-actors who propose them, each as vividly expressive as possible. The protagonist is invited to consider the additional images and accept or reject them as he chooses. Those he accepts are brought into the performance space to join the others he has already created. There may be several of them; it is helpful, however, to retain some people as observers rather than direct participants.

– Identification, recognition and resonance

➤ Since those spect-actors who have been sculpted into images are of course not simply 'material' but human beings with their own feelings and attitudes, they can be asked at this point if they can identify with the desire they have been chosen to express. Boal states that in order to be able to dynamise desires effectively,the spect-actors must feel strongly about them. Usefully, he suggests three levels of engagement that are likely to prove productive: identification, recognition and resonance (Boal 1995: 68–9). 'Identification' implies that the spect-actor believes she knows this desire from personal experience. 'Recognition' is a step further away; the spect-actor does not see herself in the image, but feels that it is nevertheless familiar to her from her knowledge of another, or others. 'Resonance' is even subtler; here, it is as if the spect-actor senses something important in the image, even though she may not consciously recognise it. However, if the spect-actor experiences none of these – if in fact she feels ignorant of or alienated from the image into which she has been sculpted – she is unlikely to be able to 'play' that desire with any authenticity. In this case, the workshop leader may ask if the image has more significance for someone else present. If so, he will take on that representation. If no one identifies with it to any degree, it may have to be rejected for the time being.

– Constellation

➤ Once the desires have been selected, the protagonist is invited to arrange them around himself in the scene as if in a constellation. He may choose to place closest to him the desires he believes are most powerful; they may be behind or beside him, or between himself and his wife. Those desires that he sees as dormant or barely acknowledged – perhaps those of which he is even somewhat ashamed – might be placed at a greater distance. All of these are expressed in the images as sculpted: so one might be standing, another on the floor, a third turning its back, and so on. Those observing are invited to comment on the protagonist's arrangement. As before, their role is not to judge it but simply to say what it is that they see. Does anything about the protagonist's choices surprise them, for instance? How does the constellation compare with their own experience of the scene as first presented? Upon hearing the spect-actors' responses the protagonist may choose to rearrange the desires, if he wishes.

– Improvisation

➤ The protagonist removes all the desires from the scene and lines them up alongside the performance space. In this stage of the exercise, the aim is to understand more about the nature and power of the protagonist's diverse impulses. In essence, the actress representing the wife replays the scene but this time the protagonist's role is taken by each desire in turn. These new 'protagonists' are not fully psychological characters but are only that desire and can only act in accordance with it; the desire which longs to hold on to his wife jealously and possessively knows only this feeling. This means that in one version of the scene the protagonist will be voluble and argumentative, in another he will be bitter, in another 'rational', in another grief-stricken. He may be silent. He may walk out of the scene altogether. In each case the actress playing the wife must improvise her response, as with Forum interventions; her intentions remain the same, but her 'text' will necessarily change. The original protagonist observes the scene as it is replayed by each desire, along with the other spect-actors. At any time he may halt the action. If he feels frustrated by the progress – or lack of progress – of one of his desires, he may withdraw it and substitute another.

– Re-constellation

➤ Once each desire has had its turn the protagonist, with the help of the spect-actors, is given the opportunity to consider what has occurred. He re-examines the constellation of images he initially created: having seen the impact of each desire when given free rein, he may want to make some adjustments. How did he feel as each one took the stage – relieved, disturbed, ashamed? How did the actress playing his wife respond to them? What did the spect-actors observe, from their vantage point? The aim of this discussion is to move towards a better understanding of the encounter and the complex feelings it provoked. Which of the protagonist's desires made him stronger and which weakened him? Why did this seem to be so? The protagonist is invited to make changes to the constellation if he wishes. On reflection he might decide to bring to the fore desires that were distanced in the first version, or vice versa.

– Re-improvisation: the antagonist faces all desires simultaneously

➤ The scene is played again, but in this version all the desires are onstage together. They can gesture, move and speak at the same time as each other, but not *to* each other. The antagonist responds to them as if they were all one person. She may address them collectively, tackle them one by one, or concentrate on some and ignore others. The protagonist and spect-actors observe closely, so that once the scene concludes – or is stopped – they are able to give detailed feedback on what took place. In this stage of the exercise it is the antagonist who becomes the principal focus. What choices did she make, when faced with all the desires? Which ones pulled her attention, which did she refuse to deal with? Where did she seem certain and where hesitant?

– Developments and variations

➤ At this stage of the exercise, several options exist. The protagonist might want to replay the original scene himself, this time ready to voice his own desires in dialogue with his wife. They might like to be given The three wishes (Exercise 4.15, p. 125) to transform the reality into the ideal of each.

➤ A further possibility, which hints at the complexity and infinite possibility of the Rainbow of Desire techniques, is for a kaleido-scope of images to be formed around the *antagonist*. In this example the actress playing the wife is not representing her own experience, but she will nevertheless have feelings about her role, and the spect actors will also be aware that this character's emotions and desires are as multilayered as those of the protagonist. In the same way as before, a series of her desires can be sculpted. Ideally, there will be enough people present for these to be created while still retaining those images that represented the desires of the protag-onist. This means that, rather than repeat the procedure described above whereby one character – here, the protagonist – faces each of the antagonist's desires one by one, it is possible to split the group up to allow multiple, simultaneous pairings: a desire of one plays the scene with a desire of the other. In this type of exercise, rather than finding a partner at random Boal suggests that '[e]ach image seeks, in subjective fashion, its own complement' (1995: 98). This recalls the openness of the provocations in Take your place (Exercise 4.12, p. 119); there is no right answer, but only one that feels right at the time. As these strange, heightened scenes are played out – as 'guilt' interacts with 'longing', for instance – each is watched by a spect-actor who serves as a witness. This role is important, since the presence of the observer reinforces a sense of theatre; she can also offer a more distanced perspective than the actors when all report back on what took place. While these scenes are occurring, the original protagonist and antagonist can move around the room, watching all couples. Once this stage has been concluded, there will need to be opportunity for reflection in each sub-group. Following this the protagonist or others may ask for certain scenes to be replayed for everyone to observe, but the exercise as a whole should finish with collective discussion.

CLOSURE

How a Theatre of the Oppressed workshop concludes will very much depend on the material the participants have produced. Boal writes that the sessions never end,

> since the objective is not to close a cycle, to generate a catharsis, or to end a development. On the contrary, its objective is to encourage autonomous activity, to set a process in motion, to stimulate transformative creativity, to change spectators into protagonists.
>
> (Boal 1992: 245)

Some theatre processes suggest leaving your work behind you when you quit the rehearsal room, symbolically or actually. Boal insists that you take it with you. A whole group or small group discussion in the last part of a workshop could be channelled towards a consideration of how this might happen. Sometimes the session will stimulate ideas for further theatre events: a Forum show in a new context or a piece of Invisible Theatre, for example. At other times the areas identified as ripe for transformation will be individual, behavioural. Participants can be invited to reflect upon this and, if they wish, to share their thoughts.

All theatre processes are demanding, since theatre by its nature requires a degree of individual exposure and self-examination. Theatre of the Oppressed need not be considered more challenging or revealing than other methods, but one should be aware of its specific pressures. Many exercises invite participants to recall and express memories that may be painful. What happens if someone is disturbed, even trauma-tised, by the experience of the workshop? As I noted early in the chapter, it is important to be aware of and sensitive to the possibility of this occurring. Again, it is helpful to incorporate safeguards. In my experience, problems are most likely to occur if the necessity for this is overlooked, if someone is urged to share something she might sooner keep private, or if a contribution is ignored or wilfully misinterpreted. How exercises are set up is a key factor, as is timing – it is easy to invite more material than can possibly be examined, but this may not itself be a problem as long as participants understand the structure and direction of the session. And sometimes even catharsis can be helpful, as Boal has acknowledged in later writings. The catharsis of Theatre of the Oppressed is not a process that purges the desire to take action, he insists, but one that removes those blocks that *inhibit* action (1995: 72–3). And contrary to what he writes in this passage it might, I think, be appropriate for a session occasionally to end in calm rather than disequilibrium: not the calm of resignation or passivity, but of a balanced readiness from which it is possible to move forward.

GLOSSARY

Bertolt Brecht 6

Bertolt Brecht (1898–1956) was a German playwright, director and dramaturg whose ideas have exercised enormous influence on contemporary Western theatre, perhaps principally in the popularisation of anti-illusionistic staging methods. Most significant in terms of his impact on Boal are his theories of and experiments in Epic Theatre.

conscientização 19

Term connected with the educational work of Paulo Freire. *Conscientização*, or consciousness-raising, refers to the process of learning to recognise the social or class basis underlying 'individual' desires, attitudes and actions.

Cop in the Head 24

Term used by Boal to suggest that the restrictive forces inhibiting freedom of action can sometimes be inside our own heads rather than deriving from external oppressors. The Rainbow of Desire techniques, particularly, aim to identify these 'cops' and search for ways to dislodge them.

Epic Theatre 6

This term was applied by Brecht to describe certain tendencies within German avant-garde theatre of the 1920s and, later, his own practice. Brecht's Epic Theatre is principally characterised by sociopolitical subject-matter, appeal to reason rather than emotion, and deliberate highlighting of the drama as foreknown narrative as opposed to unfolding spontaneous action. Boal's work draws directly and self-consciously on these ideas. The term did not originate with Brecht, however. Aristotle discusses 'Epic' poetry, referring to a narrative that is not bound by unities of time and place. Additionally, Brecht's contemporary Erwin Piscator termed 'Epic' his own experiments in theatrical form, which fluidly incorporated documentary material and film projection into the presentation of dramatic action. Boal acknowledges this diversity of usage.

Forum Theatre 2

Theatre of the Oppressed method in which a scene demonstrating an oppression is presented by actors and then replayed with spontaneous interventions by audience members who replace the protagonist. The aim is twofold: to find ways to combat a specific oppression, and to create maximum opportunity for participation.

Image Theatre 21

Core techniques of Theatre of the Oppressed based around use of the body to express themes, emotions and attitudes. Participants use their own bodies or 'sculpt' the bodies of others to articulate the chosen subject. Image Theatre techniques are (at least initially) non-verbal.

Invisible Theatre 21

Theatre of the Oppressed technique whereby a prepared scene or action addressing an important issue of social concern is played in a public context as if it was a real (i.e. non-theatrical) event. Invisible Theatre seeks to provoke reactions from and debate among spectators, who remain unaware that what they have witnessed is a piece of drama.

Joker 14

A compère figure within Theatre of the Oppressed practices, whose function is to mediate between actors and spectators and in all ways possible assist the latter's participation within the dramatic action. Boal has described the Joker as a 'midwife' whose task is to facilitate, but not control, the theatre event. The idea for a Joker system first emerged with the Arena Theatre's 1965 production of *Zumbi*, but has been modified since its initial proposal.

Legislative Theatre 25

Ongoing project developed in 1993 by the CTO-Rio, when Boal was elected Vereador (Member of the Legislative Chamber) for Rio de Janeiro. Legislative Theatre aims to 'theatricalise politics' by establishing a direct line of communication between Theatre of the Oppressed explorations at grass-roots level and an actual law-making process.

Newspaper Theatre 21

Theatre of the Oppressed method using daily news items as the basis for theatrical performance, in the process examining and exposing the 'mediation' of events by the newspapers themselves. This method can be traced back to the 1930s' Living Newspaper experiments of the Federal Theater Project in the US, although Boal does not acknowledge direct influence.

praxis 38

Term used by Paulo Freire and others to refer to a model of thinking, learning and doing in which theory and practice are not discrete concepts but are recognised as interdependent and inseparable: theory is grounded in action, and action is theory embodied.

Rainbow of Desire 24

Umbrella term for the body of Theatre of the Oppressed techniques, developed by Boal when working in Europe, used to explore issues which appear to be more individual/psychological in emphasis than social/political. Rainbow of Desire has often been compared with psychodrama, the method of therapeutic theatre developed earlier in the century by Austrian practitioner Jacob Moreno.

Simultaneous Dramaturgy 5

Theatre of the Oppressed technique whereby spectators choose a theme or story to be improvised by the actors. The technique

is so called because the spectators' 'playwrighting' is given immediate practical realisation on stage.

spect–actor 42

Boal's term for the spectator-turned-actor, the participatory role
sought by Theatre of the Oppressed that involves both reflection
and active intervention.

Konstantin Stanislavsky 6

Konstantin Stanislavsky (1863–1938) was a Russian actor, director
and teacher. He created a 'System' of acting which has become
the most widely practised method within Western theatre. Stanislavsky's training required actors to draw on their personal experience and emotions, as well as their imagination, in rehearsing a
role. He sought to combat artificiality and posturing, looking to
achieve 'truth' in performance. His work has been principally
associated with realist drama and for this reason is often represented, over-simplistically, as a polar opposite of Brecht's. Boal
has great admiration for both practitioners. While his borrow-
ings from Brecht are immediately evident, he is also influenced
by Stanislavsky, especially in the emphasis upon exploring the
complexities of an actor's inner life.

BIBLIOGRAPHY

WORKS BY BOAL

Boal, Augusto (1979) *Theatre of the Oppressed*, trans. C. and M.-O. Leal McBride, London: Pluto Press.

Boal, Augusto (1992) *Games for Actors and Non-Actors*, trans. A. Jackson, London: Routledge.

Boal, Augusto (1995) *The Rainbow of Desire: The Boal Method of Theatre and Therapy*, trans. A. Jackson, London: Routledge.

Boal, Augusto (1998) *Legislative Theatre*, trans. A. Jackson, London: Routledge.

Boal, Augusto (2001) *Hamlet and the Baker's Son: My Life in Theatre and Politics*, trans. A. Jackson and C. Blaker, London: Routledge.

INTERVIEWS

Driskell, Charles B. (1975) 'An Interview with Augusto Boal', *Latin American Theatre Review* 9(1): 71–8.

Heritage, Paul (2002) '"The Crossing of Many Cultures": An Interview with Augusto Boal', in David Bradby and Maria Delgado (eds) *The Paris Jigsaw: Internationalism and the City's Stages*, Manchester: Manchester University Press, 153–66.

Paterson, Douglas and Weinberg, Mark (1996) 'In His Own Words: An Interview with Augusto Boal about the Theatre of the Oppressed'. Online, available at: http://www.artswire.org/Community/highperf/hp/hpmags/HP72texts/Boal1.html (accessed 28 March 2002).

Taussig, Michael and Schechner, Richard (1990) 'Boal in Brazil, France, the USA: An Interview with Augusto Boal', *The Drama Review* 34(3): 50–65.

CRITICISM

ON BOAL AND THEATRE OF THE OPPRESSED

Anderson, Robert (1996) 'The Muses of Chaos and Destruction of *Arena conta Zumbi*', *Latin American Theatre Review* 29(2): 15–28.

Babbage, Frances (ed.) (1995) *Working Without Boal: Digressions and Developments in the Theatre of the Oppressed*, special issue of *Contemporary Theatre Review* 3(1).

Campbell, Ali (1995) 'Questions from Rio', *Contemporary Theatre Review* 3(1): 109–19.

Davis, David and O'Sullivan, Carmel (2000) 'Boal and the Shifting Sands: The Un-Political Master Swimmer', *New Theatre Quarterly* 16(3): 288–97.

Feldhendler, Daniel (1994) 'Augusto Boal and Jacob L. Moreno: Theatre and Therapy', in Jan Cohen-Cruz and Mady Schutzman (eds) *Playing Boal: Theatre, Therapy, Activism*, London: Routledge, 87–109.

Ganguly, Sanjoy (2001) 'From the Battlefield', *Metaxis: The Theatre of the Oppressed Review* 1(1): 34–5.

George, David (1995) 'Theatre of the Oppressed and Teatro de Arena: In and Out of Context', *Latin American Theatre Review* 28(2): 39–54.

Heritage, Paul (1994) 'The Courage to be Happy: Augusto Boal, Legislative Theatre, and the 7th International Festival of the Theatre of the Oppressed', *The Drama Review* 38(3): 25–34.

Heritage, Paul (1998) 'The Promise of Performance: True Love/Real Love', in Richard Boon and Jane Plastow (eds) *Theatre Matters: Performance and Culture on the World Stage*, Cambridge: Cambridge University Press, 154–76.

Heritage, Paul (2001) 'Theatre in Prisons', *Metaxis: The Theatre of the Oppressed Review* 1(1): 32–3.

Kershaw, Baz (2001) 'Review of *Legislative Theatre*', *Theatre Research International* 26(2): 218–19.

Luzuriaga, Gerardo (1990) 'Augusto Boal and his Poetics of the Oppressed', *Discurso: Revista de Estudios Ibero-Americanos* 8(1): 53–66.

McCoy, Ken (1995) 'Liberating the Latin American Audience: The *Conscientização* of Enrique Buenaventura and Augusto Boal', *Theatre Insight* 6(2): 10–16.

Milleret, Margo (1987) 'Acting into Action: Teatro Arena's *Zumbi*', *Latin American Theatre Review* 21(1): 19–27.

Milling, Jane and Ley, Graham (2001) *Modern Theories of Performance*, Houndsmill: Palgrave.

Paterson, Doug (1994) 'A Role to Play for the Theatre of the Oppressed', *The Drama Review* 38(3): 37–49.

Pellarolo, Silvia (1994) 'Transculturating Postmodernism? Augusto Boal's Theater Practice Across Cultural Boundaries', *Gestos: Teoria y Practica del Teatro Hispanico* 9(17): 199–212.

Santos, Barbara (2001) 'The CTO-Rio: A Different World is Possible', *Metaxis: The Theatre of the Oppressed Review* 1(1): 6–10.

Schutzman, Mady and Cohen-Cruz, Jan (eds) (1994) *Playing Boal: Theatre, Therapy, Activism*, London: Routledge.

GENERAL

Albuquerque, Severino João (1989) 'From "Abertura" to "Nova República": Politics and the Brazilian Theater of the Late Seventies and Eighties', *Hispanofila* 96: 87–95.

Andersen, Øivind and Haarberg, Jon (2001) *Making Sense of Aristotle: Essays in Poetics*, London: Duckworth.

Aristotle (1995) *Politics*, ed. R.F. Stalley, trans. E. Barker, Oxford: Oxford University Press.

Aristotle (1996a) *Poetics*, ed. and trans. M. Heath, Harmondsworth: Penguin.

Aristotle (1996b) *The Nicomachean Ethics*, ed. and trans. S. Watt, Ware: Wordsworth.

Bellos, Alex (2003) 'Everybody Wants a Brazilian . . .', *Observer* 'Review', 6 July 2003, 10.

Belsey, Catherine (1985) *The Subject of Tragedy*, London: Methuen.

Bethell, Leslie (1994) *On Democracy in Brazil Past and Present*, London: Institute of Latin American Studies.

Cattanach, Ann (1992) *Drama for People With Special Needs*, London: A & C Black.

Eagleton, Terry (1976) *Marxism and Literary Criticism*, London: Methuen.

Esslin, Martin (1980) *Brecht: A Choice of Evils*, London: Eyre Methuen.

Fortier, Mark (1997) *Theory/Theatre*: London: Routledge.

Freire, Paulo (1972) *Pedagogy of the Oppressed*, Harmondsworth: Penguin.

Gassner, John (1954) 'Modern Playwriting at the Crossroads', in A.L. Bader (ed.) (1965) *To the Young Writer*, Ann Arbor: University of Michigan Press, 17–32.

Gassner, John (1956) *Form and Idea in Modern Theatre*, New York: Yale University Press.

George, David (1992) *The Modern Brazilian Stage*, Austin: University of Texas Press.

Halliwell, Stephen (1986) *Aristotle's Poetics,* London: Duckworth.

Happé, Peter (1999) *English Drama Before Shakespeare*, London: Longman.

Hegel, Georg W.F. (1920) *The Philosophy of Fine Art: Vol. 4*, ed. and trans. F.P.B. Osmaston, London: G. Bell & Sons Ltd.

Honderich, Ted (ed.) (1995) *The Oxford Companion to Philosophy*, Oxford: Oxford University Press.

Macfarlane, Alan (1978) *The Origins of English Individualism*, Oxford: Basil Blackwell.

Machiavelli, Niccolò (1979) 'The Mandrake Root', in *The Portable Machiavelli*, ed. and trans. P. Bondanella and M. Musa, Harmondsworth: Penguin, 430–79.

McLellan, David (ed.) (1977) *Karl Marx: Selected Writings*, Oxford: Oxford University Press.

Marx, Karl and Engels, Friedrich (1992) *The Communist Manifesto*, ed. D. McLellan, Oxford: Oxford University Press.

Maus, Katharine Eisaman (1995) *Inwardness and Theater in the English Renaissance*, Chicago: University of Chicago Press.

Milleret, Margo (1990a) 'Pedagogy and Popular Art for the Masses from the CPC', *Brasil/Brazil* 3(3): 18–31.

Milleret, Margo (1990b) '(Re)Playing the Brazilian Dictatorship', *Discurso: Revista de Estudios Iberamericanos* 7(1): 213–24.

Mind the Gap and ADA Inc. (2001) *Includeo: Audience Development Programme Report* (Spring 2001), Bradford: Mind the Gap.

Rorty, Amélie Oksenberg (ed.) (1992) *Essays on Aristotle's Poetics*, Princeton: Princeton University Press.

Singer, Peter (2001) *Hegel*, Oxford: Oxford University Press.

Walker, Greg (ed.) (2000) *Medieval Drama: An Anthology*, Oxford: Blackwell.

Weinoldt, Kirsten (2001) 'Stage Struck II: Milestones of Brazilian Theater in the 20th Century', *Brazzil*. Online, available at: http://www.brazzil.com (accessed 23 May 2002).

Willett, John (ed.) (1964) *Brecht on Theatre*, London: Methuen.

Williams, Raymond (1977) *Marxism and Literature*, Oxford: Oxford University Press.

INDEX

ROUTLEDGE STUDY GUIDES